CU00949673

Gnostic Trends in the Local Church

Gnostic Trends in the Local Church

The Bull in Christ's China Shop

MICHAEL W. PHILLIBER

RESOURCE *Publications* • Eugene, Oregon

GNOSTIC TRENDS IN THE LOCAL CHURCH
The Bull in Christ's China Shop

Copyright © 2011 Michael W. Philliber. All rights reserved. Except
for brief quotations in critical publications or reviews, no part of
this book may be reproduced in any manner without prior written
permission from the publisher. Write: Permissions, Wipf and Stock
Publishers, 199 W. 8th Ave., Suite 3, Eugene, OR 97401.

Resource Publications
An Imprint of Wipf and Stock Publishers
199 W. 8th Ave., Suite 3
Eugene, OR 97401
www.wipfandstock.com

ISBN 13: 1-978-1-61097-414-1
Manufactured in the U.S.A.

All scripture quotations, unless otherwise indicated, are taken from
the New King James Version®. Copyright © 1982 by Thomas Nelson,
Inc. Used by permission. All rights reserved.

*Dedicated to my longsuffering,
gracious Anna*

and

*Providence Presbyterian Church
(PCA) of Midland Texas.*

Contents

Preface

As you, the reader, prepare to delve into this book, I must state three important items to keep in mind. First, I have drawn from a number of sources. Though I have learned a great deal from many of these authors, my quoting them should not be taken as a blanket approval of everything they have written. I simply find them helpful on this issue. I have also been amazed at how universal the problem of Gnosticism is. The concerns voiced by the quoted authors come from every segment of the Christian tribe: Roman Catholic, Anglican, Protestant, and Eastern Orthodox. Therefore the authors I have drawn from should be seen as reflecting the universality of the concern, not my global approval of their works.

Second, I have written from within my own arm of the larger Christian community. I am a pastor within the Presbyterian Church in America and made specific vows at my ordination that govern the parameters of what I teach and believe. I take those vows seriously. That being said, I hope that the reader will be pleased with my upfront declaration and not feel put out by it. I honestly believe that other traditions can gain from this material and fit it within their own doctrinal standards.

Finally, I am assuming that most of the readers will be leaders in their churches. Therefore I write this book with them in mind. That should help to explain the semitechnical language that crops up on occasion, and why the final section is written mostly from the angle of the church leadership.

Acknowledgments

I AM grateful for the people of Providence Presbyterian Church (PCA), along with the leadership. They have been such a joy to me during this time. If I were not the pastor, I would gladly become a member of this congregation!

My deepest appreciation goes to my wife Anna for her encouragement in this project and my studies. For thirty-one years we have walked through many trials and joys, and she has never complained (well, almost never). This book is a memorial in honor of her and her devotion to our marriage.

Finally, my chief aim throughout this study has always been the words found in the first question and answer of the "Westminster Shorter Catechism": To glorify God, and to enjoy Him forever.

Introduction

In the Beginning

WHAT POSSESSED me to take up this book? There were several factors involved. Seen by themselves, none of these would normally amount to much, but piled together they stirred up a growing concern in me. Below is a description of some of those components.

First came the popular book written by Dan Brown, *The Da Vinci Code*, along with the movie based on that book. Then arrived the short-lived but much glamorized publication *The Gospel of Judas*. These two events spawned several conversations among myself, the people in my congregation, and many others around town. Those discussions covered the validity of the Gospel accounts of Jesus, what makes *The Gospel of Judas* categorically different from the New Testament Gospels, and whether there was any truth to *The Da Vinci Code*. For example, not long after Brown's book came out, I overheard some women in our congregation describing how a few the ladies in their quilting club spoke highly of *The Da Vinci Code* and asserted that it was historically accurate.

I also observed an interesting phenomenon in our particular city in West Texas during this time. After making several trips to the local franchise bookstore, I watched as, month by month, the Christian section got overrun by books from pro-gnostic authors like Elaine Pagels and Marvin Meyer. Over the next few years I frequented the local used bookstores to see if any copies of Elaine Pagels's books or *The Da Vinci Code* were cycling through. I made repeated trips to these used bookstores from 2004 to 2010, and I noted that there seemed to be no perceivable movement once the books got into consumers' hands. In other words, the books were selling at the franchise stores, and after six months to six years, they were not showing up at used bookstores. Unlike *The Purpose-Driven Life* and the *Left Behind* series, which were showing up in large quantities, these modern gnostic books seemed to be staying in peoples' homes.[1] That may mean nothing, or it may mean that people are holding onto these books because they value them. If the latter is true, then this gnostic drift is not likely to be a short-lived fad.

There was another disconcerting component thrown into this mix. I kept running across people who claimed to be Christians but made statements like, "I'm not into organized religion, but I'm a very spiritual person." When I probed them, they would explain that what mattered to them was not the church organization, but their own, very personal experience of God. The trappings of "religion," church leaders, church history, and liturgy were optional.

---

1. At one used bookstore I found, on one visit, forty copies of *The Purpose-Driven Life* and around twenty-seven copies of the first book in the *Left Behind* series. But there were no copies of *The Da Vinci Code*, any copies of *The Gnostic Bible*, or any others of that genre.

Their single emphasis was on themselves and their own personal sense of experiencing the divine.

During the same time period I had several disturbing discussions with churchgoing Christians from around town. It increasingly became clear to me that many believers did not seem prepared to answer the challenges made against the historical and authoritative reliability of the canonical Gospels and the deity of Christ. A significant number of them struggled with how to answer the objections popularized by *The Da Vinci Code* and *The Gospel of Judas*.

Then in 2007 I ran into what appeared, at first, to be an unrelated source but ultimately certified my growing unease. Christian Smith had recently completed a well-researched survey of religious teenagers in America. He cuts across denominational, ethnic, liberal–conservative, and religious lines in his investigation. His final analysis of the reigning religion in America validates my concern that gnostic tendencies have a powerful influence in our congregations. For as he notes:

> a particular religious outlook that is distinct from traditional faith commitments of most historical U. S. religious traditions, what we are calling Moralistic Therapeutic Deism, appears to have established a significant foothold among very many contemporary U.S. teenagers. . . . It may be the new mainstream American religious faith for our culturally post-Christian, individualistic, mass-consumer capitalist society.[2]

2. Smith and Denton, *Soul Searching*, 262.

Smith further notes that "in most cases teenage religion and spirituality in the United States are much better understood as largely reflecting the world of adult religion, especially parental religion, and are in strong continuity with it."[3] The point should be obvious. What appears to be a significant outlook among American teenagers is being absorbed, primarily, from their parents. This particular religious outlook that Smith has found fits the gnostic drift. The distant, detached deity is not concerned about liberating people from sin and its destructive, cosmic effects, but about people feeling good, happy, secure, and at peace.[4] And this form of Deism lays out techniques for successfully apprehending those therapeutic goals.

Finally, I decided to do my doctoral thesis on gnostic trends in the local church. While doing my thesis I determined to see if other churches had a problem with gnostic inclinations, and so I surveyed three local congregations. The outcome showed that whether the church was Anglican, Independent, or Presbyterian, modern aspects of Gnosticism were cropping up in definitely harmful ways.

Based on the above-mentioned indicators, I felt that I needed to help the people of my congregation answer the numerous questions posed by modern Gnosticism through a couple of ways. One was to preach a series of Advent sermons on the historical aspects of Jesus' story. I purchased large quantities of the booklet *The Case for Christmas* by Lee Strobel. Copies were passed out on the first Sunday of Advent, and then I preached four sermons on successive Sundays, addressing many of the apologetic issues raised by

3. Ibid., 170.
4. Ibid., 164–65.

Strobel. As I went through the basic validity of the canonical Gospels, several congregants responded as if they had never heard any of this evidence before.[5] These responses encouraged me to do a summer adult class series at our church. The course was specifically aimed at Gnosticism's rejection of the historical and authoritative reliability of the canonical Gospels and the unequaled deity of the Christ of faith and history.[6]

As a consequence of these experiences, I have become more attuned to the fact that there is an important call for laypeople, church leaders, and ministers to: (1) recognize gnostic trends in their congregation; (2) understand what Gnosticism's main tenets are; (3) become alert to the biblical and early Christian ways to combat Gnosticism; and (4) take steps to counter these gnostic tendencies apologetically, theologically, and practically.

My desire throughout this little book is that ministers, elders, and congregations might "have their senses exercised to discern both good and evil."[7] By seeing how subtle gnostic tendencies are and ways in which to counteract those trends, others might be better prepared to detect the challenges to the Jesus Christ of history and doctrine, and to answer those objections with confidence. This book is an endeavor to help pastors and congregations take these steps.

5. Strobel, 13–54.

6. The lessons can be found in Appendix C, ready for use by church leaders in their congregations.

7. Heb 5:14.

1

Gnosticism

"A faith that discards history . . . really turns into 'Gnosticism.' It leaves flesh, incarnation—just what true history is—behind."[1]

To get a sense of Gnosticism in a brief view,[2] it might be helpful to ask the four worldview questions described by N. T. Wright: Who are we? Where are we? What is wrong? What is the solution?[3] I will also add to these questions a short discussion on alternative authorities. By asking these questions, the reader can get a clearer view of the breadth of Gnosticism and a sense of its intricate network of ideas. More important for our purpose, asking these questions will help us to see more keenly the ways in which gnostic trends are cropping up in our churches.

---

1. Benedict, *Jesus of Nazareth*, 228.

2. "Gnosis" is the Greek word for knowledge. It is used a number of times in the New Testament in a positive light. But Gnosticism was the name given to this particular heresy, very early on, because it elevated a secret knowledge over any publicly accessible knowledge.

3. Wright, *New Testament*, 121–37.

WHO ARE WE?

In Gnosticism's view the created order is the work of a lesser divinity, and the creation of our human physicality is the work of the Archons.[4] Because creation is a result of a precosmic fall, we are imprisoned creatures. This all simply means that the Archons created our humanity in order to keep the divine substance of the *pneuma* (spirit) captive.[5] This "We're trapped divinities" theme becomes a key point in the gnostic schema, especially when referring to the relationship between humans and Christ. In Elaine Pagels's approving words:

> What differentiated [the gnostics from orthodox Christians] was the level of their understanding. Uninitiated Christians mistakenly worshiped the creator, as if he were God; they believed in Christ as the one who would save them from sin, and who they believed had risen bodily from the dead: they accepted him by faith, but without understanding the mystery of his nature—or their own. But those who had gone on to receive gnosis had come to recognize Christ as the one sent from the Father of truth, whose coming revealed to them that their own nature was identical with his—and with God's.[6]

Pagels's assertion means that Christ is no more divine than we are. In other words our natures are identical, so that

4. These are the mythical powers that rule over the world under the demiurge or creator God; see Jonas, *Gnostic Religion*, 236–37; Ehrman, "Christianity Turned," 84–85.

5. Jonas, *Gnostic Religion*, 44.

6. Pagels, *Gnostic Gospels*, 116.

when we achieve gnosis we find that we are really Christ's twin. This brings Pagels to point out that once we achieve gnosis, we no longer need to see ourselves as Christians, but as Christ.[7] By pursuing this gnostic version of the divine, Pagels has thrown out the otherness of God, the *I–Thou* distinctive, so that the gnostic can now say, *I am Thou*.[8] In this way Gnosticism strips Christ of "being the eternal Son of God," who "became man, and so was, and continueth to be, God and man, in two distinct natures, and one person forever."[9] Consequently, as Pope Benedict XVI observes, Gnosticism offers a

> Completely antirationalist pattern of religion, a modern "mysticism": the absolute is, not something to be believed in, but something to be experienced. . . . Religion means bringing my self into tune with the cosmic whole, the transcending of all divisions.[10]

To summarize this point, Gnosticism holds that we—more specifically, the internal part of us—are divinities imprisoned in these bodies. It asserts we are as divine as Christ. What we need is not salvation, but gnosis, secret knowledge that will enlighten us to who we really are and give us a true knowledge that will set our minds free to be what we are, to "escape everything except the self," to "escape from the world into the self."[11]

7. Ibid., 134.
8. Pagels, *Beyond Belief*, 75.
9. "Westminster Shorter Catechism," 21.
10. Benedict, *Truth and Tolerance*, 127.
11. Peterson, *Christ Plays*, 61.

WHERE ARE WE?

Gnosticism goes further and declares that our existence is hedged in by a marred creation, a creation that feeds an alienation between "The Father of truth" and humankind. At first this sounds similar to Christianity's claim that we are alienated by sin, and all creation with us. But on further reading, it becomes clear that something else is in mind. "The universe, the domain of the Archons, is like a vast prison whose innermost dungeon is the earth, the scene of man's life."[12] The cosmos in which we live was created by the demiurge rather than the supreme God. This demiurge is often equated with the rough-and-tumble God of the Old Testament. Therefore, when Gnostics refer to the Creator, they are referring to *a lesser god.* Also in their framework, the Old Testament God is completely different from the God revealed by Jesus in the New Testament.

In a nutshell, to answer "Where are we?," the gnostic arrangement claims that creation is the result of rebellion; "a deep metaphysical alienation" is built into the creation. [13] Thus the God of the Hebrews, the God of the Old Testament who made creation, must not be such a good chap after all. In fact, there is another God, a good God, who is far removed from creation and created things. This leads to the answer for the next question, "What is wrong?"

12. Jonas, *Gnostic Religion*, 43.
13. Peterson, *Christ Plays*, 61.

WHAT IS WRONG?

Ancient and modern Gnosticism share several common themes which define them. Hans Jonas designates one of these major themes as a "dualistic-anticosmic spirit."[14]. For the gnostic, the original fall does not come after the arrival of a good creation, but occurs before it; hence the created order is a consequence of the fall.[15] This underlies Jonas's observation: "Gnosticism has been the most radical embodiment of dualism ever to have appeared on the stage of history. . . . It is a split between self and world, man's alienation from nature, the metaphysical devaluation of nature, the cosmic solitude of the spirit and the nihilism of mundane norms."[16]

Therefore the good and pure God is not the cause of creation. That means, "The solution of the gnostic type—ancient, medieval and modern—is to remove from God (or from the God beyond God) the stigma of Creation."[17] To divorce God from creation, the Gnostics argue for a series of devolving emanations (Archons, aeons, etc.) from which came a divine being, who is far distant from God, who created the cosmos in rebellion (the demiurge). As one Valentinian writing describes it: "Because of this, error became strong. But she worked on her material substance vainly, because she did not know the truth. She assumed

14. Jonas, *Gnostic Religion*, 33. In my experience, this anticosmic dualism is one of the first gnostic notions that is met with in many churches in the twenty-first century. It is seen in the devaluation of history and the physical.

15. Jonas, *Gnostic Religion*, 63.

16. Ibid., xxvi.

17. Lee, *Protestant Gnostics*, 9.

a fashioned figure while she was preparing, in power and beauty, the substitute for truth."[18]

Creation was marred from the very outset, and has imperfection programmed into its genetic fiber. According to another Valentinian "Gospel," "The world came into being through error. The agent who made it wanted it to be imperishable and immortal. He failed. He came up with less than his desire. The world was never incorruptible, nor was its maker."[19]

The result of the vast distance between God and the erroneous creation is that the gnostics are then allowed "to escape the world with impunity, for neither gnostics nor their God have any stake in it."[20] Gnostic dualism is clearly anticosmic; "The gnostic God is not merely extra-mundane and supra-mundane, but in his ultimate meaning contra-mundane."[21]

Therefore, estrangement is the key to the gnostic understanding of what is wrong. Humankind is simultaneously, along with God, alienated from the world; and yet because of the world, humankind and God are separated from one another.[22] The Archons have encased the *pneuma* (spirit) in the human body, and drugged this divine *pneuma* so that it sleeps, or stays permanently in ignorance of what it is and where it belongs. "But some of us are trapped divinities. And we need to learn how to return to our heav-

---

18. *Gospel of Truth*, 242.

19. *Gospel of Philip*, 286.

20. Lee, *Protestant Gnostics*, 9.

21. Jonas, *Gnostic Religion*, 251.

22. Jonas, *Gnostic Religion*, 326.

enly home."[23] But the Archons are barring the way so that souls that seek to climb up to God are kept from escaping the world and returning to God.[24]

Not only is there hostility from the Archons, there is also a hostile Creator God, the demiurge; "In the Gospel of Judas and other Gnostic traditions, the creator of this world is not a kind and gentle figure."[25]

All of this divine hostility is bad news for the cosmos and everyone who is within the cosmic confines. "The gnostic God is not merely extra-mundane and supra-mundane, but in his ultimate meaning contra-mundane."[26] To put it more simply, God is outside the creation, above the creation, and against the creation.

In defining what is wrong, the gnostic construction announces that creation is marred and corrupt from the very get-go. The God who is over all must be far distant from creation, and is actually working toward its demise. Finally, for the gnostic, the world is not home, but only a prison; escape is what we should want.[27] These statements direct us to hear the gnostic answer to the succeeding question, "What is the solution?"

23. Ehrman, "Christianity Turned," 87.

24. Jonas, *Gnostic Religion*, 43. I have been told by those in the know that this framework is the backbone to *Scientology*.

25. Meyer, "Gnostic Connection," 154.

26. Jonas, *Gnostic Religion*, 251.

27. Peterson, *Christ Plays*, 62.

WHAT IS THE SOLUTION?

In one way, the real goal or focus of gnostic salvation is the divine *pleroma* (fullness). "And the real object of salvation is the godhead itself, its theme the divine integrity."[28] In other words, the "ultimate salvation of what is divine in the world and humanity."[29] This salvation will come about when "all the pneumatic elements in the world have been 'formed' by knowledge and perfected."[30] The dualistic present will then collapse into a monad (single unit) of divine existence.[31] In other words, God needs saving, and when God finally gets it all together (pulls the splintered pieces of the divine back into its fullness), he will be "saved."

One of the important ways of saving God is by awakening and enlightening the divine spark within the *pneumatics* (spiritual ones). As Marvin Meyer writes in his introduction to *The Gospel of Judas*, "For gnostics, the fundamental problem in human life is not sin but ignorance, and the best way to address this problem is not through faith but through knowledge."[32]

The emphasis on gnosis (knowledge) is the essence of gnostic salvation: the "knowledge of God and the essential

---

28. Jonas, *Gnostic Religion*, 196.

29. Barnstone and Meyer, *Gnostic Bible*, 16.

30. Jonas, *Gnostic Religion*, 196.

31. Dualism is the hard division between the physical and spiritual. Most dualisms see the physical as unimportant or bad and the spiritual as better. The easiest way to say it is: "Body bad; spirit good!" You hear this dualism in statements like, "The body is the prison house or tomb of the soul."

32. Meyer, "Introduction," 7.

oneness of the self with God."[33] This saving knowledge is a direct "unmediated mystical knowledge."[34] A "secret lore, a knowledge (gnosis) that can save us from this hopeless condition."[35] In other words, to attain this knowledge there is not any need for mediation: no necessity for Bibles, no requirement for church, no demand for sacraments, no wish for ministers, just me and God!

But gnostic salvation also means that, if God is *contra-mundane* (against the creation), and if the cosmos and the created realm are a main part of the problem, then they must be escaped altogether. That is why the Jesus of *The Gospel of Judas* needs to be saved from his humanity (which is part of creation). Jesus reportedly gives permission for Judas to betray him so as to free him from his body; "But you will exceed all of them. For you will sacrifice the man that clothes me."[36] The affirming footnote that accompanies this text explains, "The death of Jesus, with the assistance of Judas, is taken to be the liberation of the spiritual person within."[37] So, if this is the case with Jesus, it is just as essential for his followers. Bart Ehrman, in his article that attends to *The Gospel of Judas*, agrees; "We are trapped here, in these bodies of flesh, and we need to learn how to escape."[38] And a little later on, he declares unapologetically, "Salvation does not come by worshiping the God of this world or accepting his creation. It comes by denying this world and rejecting

---

33. Ibid., 5.
34. Barnstone and Meyer, *Gnostic Bible*, 16.
35. Peterson, *Christ Plays*, 61.
36. *Gospel of Judas*, 43.
37. Ibid., 137.
38. Ehrman, "Christianity Turned," 84.

the body that binds us to it."[39] There will be no resurrection, since Jesus would not want to be raised from the dead, and neither should we.[40]

As we pull this final question and its answer together, it becomes clear that physicality is a tomb. The real me should want to escape and be absorbed back into the divine. In fact the real Jesus wanted to be free, and any idea of the resurrection of the body is ridiculously out of the question. Finally, what a person needs so as to be saved is to gain this powerful, secret knowledge that gives one the technique for regaining her emancipating higher consciousness. "Whatever the 'Jesus' of the Gnostic 'gospels' has done, the main thing about him is that he has come, not to rescue the world, or to heal or change it, but to give secret teaching about how to escape it."[41]

These four worldview questions help move us along, so that we can grasp a better sense of what ancient and modern Gnosticism thinks. But there is one other question which has not been asked. By what authority, or better, what are the authoritative source materials which give fuel and energy to Gnosticism?

ALTERNATIVE AUTHORITIES

Besides anticosmic dualism, there is an additional striking concept of the gnostic identification badge: the proliferation of alternative textual authorities. Elaine Pagels boasts

---

39. Ibid., 101.
40. Ibid., 110.
41. Wright, *Gospel of Jesus*, 68.

that the gnostic texts provide "a powerful alternative"[42] to orthodox Christianity.

The reason for these auxiliary sources of textual authority in gnostic circles revolves around the importance of retelling the Jewish-Christian story in anticosmic dualistic ways. Philip Lee points out:

> What is not always recognized is that before there can be a deliberate escape from the real world into an alternately designed world, there first must be a deliberate escape from the real God to an alternately designed God. This, in fact, is the gnostic trick.[43]

To get away from telling the Jewish-Christian monotheistically procosmic story, it becomes indispensable for gnostics to create other textual authorities: for example, supplemental gospels like *The Gospel of Truth* or *The Gospel of Judas*.

Gnostics may also reshape the biblical story by using a template of unique interpretations of the Christian Scriptures, as Pagels demonstrates in her two books, *The Johannine Gospel in Gnostic Exegesis* and *The Gnostic Paul: Gnostic Exegesis of the Pauline Letters*. In both instances Pagels shows how Valentinian Gnostics read the Christian Scriptures. In fact, Pagels demonstrates how gnosis was the crucial interpretive lens for the way they read all canonical Scripture. That "gnosis itself serves the Gnostics as their hermeneutical principle."[44] Also, "Heracleon shares this

---

42. Pagels, *Gnostic Gospels*, 151.

43. Lee, *Protestant Gnostics*, 9.

44. Pagels, *Gnostic Paul*, 3.

understanding of 'context.' For him, as for Ptolemy, 'gnosis,' and not the textual wording, furnishes the exegetical context."[45]

Their alternative authority can also include a mixture of both of the above options. No matter what the case may be, it is essential to have different sources of authority if another kind of Christianity is going to be forged. For Gnosticism this is critical for the purpose of disconnecting their alternate version of Christianity from any historical and creational moorings. Pope Benedict XVI points out the danger in a concisely insightful way; "If we push this history aside, Christian faith as such disappears and is recast as some other religion."[46]

THE PNEUMATIC AUTHORITY

Having alternative written and didactic authorities, however, is not enough. The gnostic claims a more primary authority: the divine *pneuma* within. "But the *pneumaticos*, 'spiritual' man, who does not belong to any objective scheme, is above the law, beyond good and evil, and a law unto himself in the power of his 'knowledge.'"[47] Pagels stresses this as well when she points out, "The disciple who comes to know himself can discover, then, what even Jesus cannot teach," and so he becomes a follower of his own mind. "He learns what he needs to know by himself in meditative silence. Consequently, he considers himself equal to everyone, maintaining his own independence of

45. Pagels, *Johannine Gospel*, 43.

46. Benedict, *Truth and Tolerance*, xv.

47. Jonas, *Gnostic Religion*, 334.

everyone else's authority."[48] That means that whoever comes to "see the Lord" by way of an inner vision "can claim that his or her own authority equals, or surpasses, that of the Twelve—and of their successors."[49] Therefore, what matters to the gnostic is not the historicity of Jesus or the historical authenticity of the canonical Gospels, nor any objective authority, but "spiritual vision."[50] The Gnostics, old and new, just happen to be "those restless, inquiring people who marked out a solitary path of self-discovery"[51] that insist on "the primacy of immediate experience."[52] To put this in a different way, the gnostic's experience becomes her own authoritative text.

SUMMARY

Though modern Gnosticism may or may not hold to a pantheon of aeons and Archons, modern Gnosticism, like ancient Gnosticism:

1. Holds to the same anticosmic dualism which strips the created order, and our physicality, of importance and value.

2. Divides the Jesus of history from the Christ of faith.[53]

3. Denigrates the historical strength and authenticity of the canonical Gospels.[54]

48. Pagels, *Gnostic Gospels*, 131–32.
49. Ibid., 13–14.
50. Ibid., 11.
51. Ibid., 149.
52. Ibid., 145.
53. Pagels, *Johannine Gospel*, 118.
54. Pagels, *Origin of Satan*, xxi–xxii.

4. Elevates unmediated individual mystical experiences between the self and the divine.[55]

5. Sees salvation as being from ignorance and creation, not from sin.[56]

6. Rehearses an anticosmic narrative in ways that are out of joint with the monotheistic, procreation, prohistory Jewish-Christian story.[57]

7. Finds final authority in the *pneuma* within the *pneumaticos*, the "spirit" within the "spiritual one."[58]

Or to put these summary points in another way,

> Gnosticism offers us spirituality without the inconvenience of creation. Gnosticism offers us spirituality without the inconvenience of sin or morality. Gnosticism offers us spirituality without the inconvenience of people we don't like or who aren't "our kind." And maybe most attractive of all, Gnosticism offers us spirituality without God, at least any god other than the spark of divinity I sense within me.[59]

This cursory review of Gnosticism's basic concepts should help to give the reader a solid feel for the danger that lies in Gnosticism, and how it sabotages the Christian faith. As this book unfolds I will bring out more of the modern connotations of Gnosticism within local churches.

---

55. Bloom, *American Religion*, 45–49.
56. Pagels, *Gnostic Paul*, 22.
57. Reno, *Genesis*, 175–79.
58. Pagels, *Gnostic Gospels*, 145.
59. Peterson, *Christ Plays*, 62.

2

Searching for Trouble

IN THE previous chapter I reviewed the basic tenets of Gnosticism, both old and new. Once I discovered some of the major gnostic ingredients, I then set out to see if any of these trends were cropping up in our local churches. To do that I assessed three congregations in our little city in West Texas, using a survey I made up that had the basic concepts of Gnosticism in mind.[1]

The three churches I reviewed were of dissimilar size and racial makeup, but all professed to be orthodox Christian churches of a more conservative bent. They were from diverse denominational traditions. One was Calvinist in its doctrine and Presbyterian in its church government, another was Baptist in its beliefs and independent in its government, and the final one was historically Reformed in theology and Episcopal in government. Two of the churches were overwhelmingly white in their racial makeup, while one had a majority of African-Americans, with a goodly number of other ethnicities.

My primary concern was to investigate the possibility that Gnosticism's anticosmic dualism might be getting

1. See Appendix A for the survey matter.

a foothold. I was especially concerned with the deprecia-tion of the historical life and value of Jesus Christ, making his death of little or no salvific worth. Simultaneous with that depreciation, there might be a greater emphasis on unmediated mystical knowledge, an existential experience that would trump legitimate outside authority. Or, because of Gnosticism's challenges to the canonical Gospels, there might be a positing of other written and hermeneutical authorities. Finally, one last trademark I looked for was an acceptance of modern Gnosticism's proposition that the Emperor Constantine and the Council of Nicea forced an intolerantly closed canon (rule or boundary) of what was "Scripture" onto the church.

I admit to not being any kind of professional statisti-cian. The questions I asked seemed to be worth asking, and the answers were worth reading. There may very well be other ways to interpret the results, but within the context of things I had been hearing, seeing, and reading among Christians, I think the conclusions get very close to the truth of what is going on within local congregations. The remainder of this chapter will not deal with the technical aspects of the survey, but with the highlights of the trends reflected in the responses.

SURVEY

Questions 1 and 2

The first two questions probed the respondents' knowledge of, and experiences with, *The Da Vinci Code*. The inten-tion behind these was to estimate the impact of the book's challenges to the Christian faith. The point was to find out how many people knew someone who had read the book, and if those acquaintances had brought forward any of its challenges. Over two thirds of the people from all three congregations knew someone who had read the book. And the acquaintances who had read it covered the spectrum of perceptions, but most recognized the book was fiction and included inaccuracies. The responses surprised me, and didn't necessarily go along with my own interactions with people who had read it.

Question 3

The questions then moved on to situations the various parishioners were likely to come across in real life. The third question presented a hypothetical scenario about a son who came home from college and made three statements that cast doubt on the historical validity of Christian claims. The respondents were asked how they would reply to their hypothetical son. The first assertion was, "The Christian teaching that *Jesus is one being with God* was forced onto Christianity only by a vote at the Council of Nicea in 325 A.D." The next doubt-casting statement was, "The biblical Gospels are really mythical retellings of Jesus by some Christians who wrote so long after the described events that they couldn't really know what happened." The final claim was, "*The Gospel According to Thomas* is just as valid in understanding Jesus as the biblical Gospels."

In reflecting on the various replies to this threefold question, I was partly encouraged but also found areas that need to be strengthened. It appeared that each congregation had some internal inconsistency. Only one congregation had a majority of people fairly well prepared to answer challenges to the canonical Gospels and the deity of Christ.

The parishioners of one of the other churches consistently responded to objections to Scripture and Christ's deity with faith statements.[2] They quoted the very sources that were being challenged without explaining why those sources were worth trusting. A significant portion of this church's congregants showed that they did have a concept of canonicity. From the answers these folks gave, it seemed that, on the one hand, most of the respondents have a healthy and high regard for Holy Scripture as the Word of God, able to answer all challenges. On the other hand, it appeared that almost no one either knew about or was comfortable talking about historical events as part of their apologetic.[3] This church was predominantly made up of African-Americans. It may be that in the African-American community the Bible is held in such high regard that nothing more is normally needed in defending the faith. The danger is that we do not live in a world that agrees. Opposition to the validity and authenticity of Scripture, as well as to Christ's deity, is coming from many directions with increasing intensity, and will eventually hit the African-American community hard. If there continues to be a paucity in the area of apologetics, including a minimal grasp of church history and historical validations of the faith, then the Christians in that com-

2. By "faith statements" I mean statements that assume the Bible's authority without explaining the reason why, or statements based on an "I believe" matrix.

3. They had almost no knowledge of the Council of Nicea in 325 AD, what issues were debated there, or its conclusions.

munity may become defenseless and unable to answer the objections.

The third congregation had some responses that stood on authoritative faith statements and others that took up historical tools to answer oppositions to the faith. It seemed clear that respondents from this church were quite willing to answer the challenges. Some had a good comprehension of the historical facts and the importance of knowing that history. Many understood the value of the canonical Gospels being written in close proximity to the time of the events they record. Yet there was still a significant portion that did not appear comfortable with using some of the apologetic tools available in the area of historical data.

Question 4

The fourth question placed the notion of the objective, historical events of Jesus over against the gnostic, antihistorical tendency to view unmediated mystical experience as primary. It was intentionally written in an either/or format to try to get a clear picture of what the respondents really thought: *Is this a true or untrue statement to you: True spiritual insight is built on and shaped by the truth which the apostles of Jesus taught, no matter what I have experienced?* The answers from all three churches fell heavily on the side that there is truth about Jesus that may cut against the grain of what one may experience. Nevertheless, there were many who specifically stated "feeling" and "experiences" as the key for "true spiritual insight."

Basically the replies displayed some divergence of thinking. Several people showed that they placed the weight of support for their "true spiritual insight" on experience instead of any outside confirmation. Many went to the other extreme and excluded experience all together. Some took what was an either/or question, and answered in a both/and fashion. The answers that relied only on experience seem to reveal that there might be a gap in their Christian growth. If my experience is the key for judging "true spiritual insight," then how can I answer someone who challenges the deity of Christ or family members who turn to *The Gospel of Thomas* for their spiritual formation?

Question 5

In the fifth question I attempted to authenticate the responses that were given in the previous question. Most of the statements in this question were taken either directly from Elaine Pagels, Marvin Meyer, Harold Bloom, or Hans Jonas, or they were a close paraphrase. Answer C was intended to be a short orthodox answer:

> *Which of the following statements do you feel are most true to you? (Circle as many as apply.):*
>
> A. *Because we are in God's image, we have a divine spark in us.*
>
> B. *We have direct access to God and don't need anything or anyone to make the way open to God for us.*
>
> C. *We can actually get to know God on His terms.*
>
> D. *I feel that God speaks to me personally and directs me in fresh ways.*
>
> E. *The body is the prison house of the soul.*

F. *More important than the historical Jesus is an encounter with the living Christ.*

G. *Having an inner vision of the Lord is just as important as the words of the New Testament.*

Overall, the answers by one of the congregations revealed plenty of consistency with their answers to question four above. The replies they made to question four were emphatic that the apostolic truth through Scripture trumps subjective experiences. Once the question came to them in the multiple forms of question five, their consistency appeared to be pretty firm. Based on their uniform answers, it appeared many of the people from this church had a clear sense of the place of Scripture as revelation from the God who is outside them. This position puts them at odds with Gnosticism, both ancient and modern.

The responses from the other two congregations presented a different set of trends. For example, in one congregation, a few respondents comprehended the New Age and gnostic leanings in these statements. Yet there was a significant portion of responses that leaned heavily toward their belief that their experience of "the living Christ" was far more important than the historical Jesus and his actions.

The third congregation appeared to have been attempting to balance their answers between an objective revelation of God and their own personal experiences. This proportionate way of knowing God is helpful when responding to someone who claims to have the gnostic *pneumatic authority*: the idea that the divinity trapped in me is my authority. Therefore, if people realize that faith is spawned by the incorruptible seed of the Word of God,[4] then there is not only an enduring anchor that can preserve them through the storms of life, but there is also a way to be able to distinguish and discern good from evil and right from wrong. Even so, some of the respondents seemed to understand the ground of their Christian faith as predominantly experiential. If that is the case, then how could they reply to someone who challenges their experience with another personal experience? What is the standard by which they could determine if one experience is right and another is wrong?

Overall, there were strong trends in each group toward a position that by God's own revelation one can come to know God and have a relationship with him. Yet there was also an equally strong tendency in each group toward a more subjective, experience-driven position.

Question 6

The final question addressed even more clearly the *extra nos*[5] aspect of the Christian faith:

> *Which of the following statements do you feel are more important for you?*
>
> *A. Jesus Christ, the Son of God, died on a cross outside of Jerusalem about 2,000 years ago.*
>
> *B. I have a real and living relationship with God.*

---

4. 1 Pet 1:23–25.
5. Outside of us.

My thought was that if the answers fall into the A category, or join A and B together, then the respondents would appear to have a good grasp of the importance of God's mighty acts in history (as recorded in sacred Scripture) as being the ground, and the gauge, of any experience they might have. But if the responses fall into the B category solely, then there is a heavily subjective, experience-ruled approach to religion.

In a very interesting turn, all the congregations sampled weighed in heavily on the side of basing personal experience on the historical actions of God in Jesus Christ. Several of those responding stated something along these lines: "Unless A is true, I could have no living relationship with God." This idea is similar to that of the Presbyterian theologian who fought for orthodox Christianity in the 1920s, J. Gresham Machen, who wrote: "According to the Christian conception, a creed is not a mere expression of the Christian experience, but on the contrary it is a setting forth of those facts upon which experience is based."[6] Yet, a prodigious number of responses came out strongly and clearly on the side of experience trumping history. For example, one person wrote, "The fact Jesus died is not as important as statement B."[7]

This development shows that some might not have grasped the importance of the historical Jesus to their salvation. Likewise, they might not be able to respond to the challenges Gnosticism raises when it divides the historical Jesus and the Christ of faith. Also, this trend was not confined to any one denomination, for all three congregations

6. Machen, *Christianity and Liberalism*, 19.
7. There were several responses that made similar claims.

showed similar signs of leaning in this way, though in vary-ing intensities. The trouble is that this movement toward elevating experience can make the faith once for all deliv-ered to the saints seem like so much bias or preference. It can neutralize a congregation's, and an individual's, ability to withstand someone else's arguments that are based on personal experiences. As Harold Bloom poignantly states in *The American Religion*, "The experiential encounter with Jesus or God is too overwhelming for memories of com-munity to abide, and the believer returns from the abyss of ecstasy with the self enhanced and otherness devalued."[8] Later he describes how this experiential faith, divorced from doctrine, replaces doctrine with "a timeless *knowing* that in itself saves."[9]

But orthodox Christianity's response to this challenge is to rehearse and embrace the truth of history and doc-trine. N. T. Wright, once Bishop of Durham, England, made this very clear in *The Challenge of Jesus*:

> If Christianity is not rooted in things that actually happened in first-century Palestine, we might as well be Buddhists, Marxists or almost anything else. And if Jesus never existed, or if he was quite different from what the Gospels and the church's worship affirms him to have been, then we are indeed living in a cloud-cuckoo-land.[10]

Machen put it succinctly: "'Christ died'—that is his-tory; 'Christ died for our sins'—that is doctrine. Without

---

8. Bloom, *American Religion*, 27.

9. Ibid., 49.

10. Wright, *Challenge of Jesus*, 18.

these two elements, joined in an absolutely indissoluble union, there is no Christianity."[11] And Pope Benedict XVI agrees with the importance of the historical nature of Christian faith as well; "A faith that discards history . . . really turns into 'Gnosticism.' It leaves flesh, incarnation—just what true history is—behind."[12]

CONCLUSION

What can be learned from these survey results? Many of the Christians I surveyed appear to hold to the Scriptures and to the historical Jesus tenaciously. Overall they seem to understand the importance of the Christian faith being, as Wright said, "rooted in things that actually happened in first-century Palestine."[13]

On the other hand, when confronted with scenarios where there are questions about the historical and au-thoritative genuineness of the canonical Gospels, they struggle. If they largely set aside the historical aspects of the Christian faith and an *extra-nos* sense of truth, then they are left without any tools to distinguish what is true from what is not. That means many Christians might be suscep-tible to the deceptive trap—especially the subtler aspects of Gnosticism—that tries to divide the historical Jesus from the Christ of faith.

11. Machen, *Christianity and Liberalism*, 27.

12. Benedict, *Jesus of Nazareth*, 228.

13. Wright, *Challenge of Jesus*, 18.

3

Biblical Theology

*"The present orthodoxy seems to be that
there is no such thing as heresy; my belief, so long as it
is sincere, is as acceptable as the next fellow's."*[1]

TERTULLIAN NOTED in his anti-Gnostic work, *The Prescriptions Against Heretics*, "Just so, heresy derives its strength from men's weakness and has none when it meets a really strong faith."[2] If Tertullian was right, then to take away the strength of modern Gnosticism would require building up the faith of God's people. Therefore, in this chapter I will display the biblical virtue of stirring up the faithful to meet the challenge of neo-Gnosticism. Next, I will describe the central place Jesus Christ holds in the strong faith. Then, I will point out the importance of re-membering the apostolic message about Jesus Christ in the strengthening of the faithful. Finally, I will show the essential environment within which believers may withstand the troublemakers. To accomplish these four ventures, it will be helpful to examine the little New Testament letter of Jude.

1. Lee, *Protestant Gnostics*, 40.
2. Tertullian, *Prescriptions*, 32.

In the letter of Jude the writer appears to be wrestling with some form of proto-Gnosticism. Jude briefly describes those who are troubling the believers, what is wrong with them, and how the faithful can move forward in withstanding them. As Edwin Blum points out in his commentary, Jude "evidently hopes that by his concise but vigorous exposure of [the troublemakers], the church will see the danger of their error and be alert to the coming judgment on it."[3]

THE BIBLICAL BASIS FOR DEFENDING
THE FAITH AGAINST NEO-GNOSTICISM

When Jude penned his short letter to the Christians, he stated that the times and circumstances mandated that he should stir them up to fight for the true faith; "I found it necessary to write to you exhorting you to contend earnestly for the faith which was once for all delivered to the saints" (v. 3). J. N. D. Kelly points out that the letter from Jude is "a peremptory exhortation" to defend the Christian faith, "directed at a particular situation."[4]

The particular situation which instigated Jude to take up the pen and write this letter were "certain men" who had gained access into the fellowship without notice and undermined the faith (v. 4). This undermining the faith manifested itself in pernicious outbreaks of misconduct and a specific renunciation of Jesus Christ the master and Lord.

These troublemakers, if not specifically gnostic, were dispensing an embryonic Gnosticism. George Ladd explains, "Jude is addressing himself to the . . . problem of

3. Blum, "Jude," 384.
4. Kelly, *Peter and Jude*, 246.

libertine Gnostics . . . and writes to encourage his readers to contend for an orthodox faith (v. 3)."[5] Also, Kelly's assessment affirms that an emerging Gnosticism is Jude's concern; "We are therefore probably justified in overhearing . . . the opening shots in the fateful struggle between the Church and Gnosticism which was to feature large in the 2nd cent."[6] Therefore, Jude was confronted with a situation analogous to our time.

One reason Jude raised the alarm was that many of those who were infiltrating the Christian communities did not want to leave the institutional structures of the church. Jude describes how they found their way into the love feasts (v. 12), causing division. Also, no matter what spiritual superiority they might have claimed for themselves, Jude describes them as the very ones who were really without the Spirit (v. 19). In his introduction to *The Scandal of the Incarnation*, Hans Urs von Balthasar observes of ancient Gnosticism what is true about some forms of the modern: "What made it so insidious was the fact that the Gnostics very often did not want to leave the Church. Instead they claimed to be offering a superior and more authentic exposition of Holy Scripture, though, of course, this was only for the 'superior souls.'"[7]

Some of the marks of the saboteurs, which Jude identifies, are: (1) Their alternative, libertine lifestyles (v. 4, 7, 8, 10, 16, 18 and 19); (2) their rebelliousness toward authorities (8–11); (3) their denial, by both word and deed, of "our only Master and our Lord Jesus Christ" (v. 4). Jude's response is

5. Ladd, *Theology*, 655.

6. Ibid., 231.

7. Irenaeus and Balthasar, *Scandal*, 1.

to challenge the faithful to take the assaults of these people seriously, and to rise up and contend for the faith.

OUR ONLY MASTER AND LORD, JESUS CHRIST

One of the first accusations Jude makes about these proto-gnostics is that they have turned God's grace into a platform for lewdness, and they have denied important aspects of the person of Jesus Christ (v. 4). Jude believes that both go hand in hand—that the proto-gnostics' poor *praxis* (behavior) is an embodiment of their poor *pistis* (belief). He designates them as "ungodly ones, who are turning the grace of our God into debauchery and are denying our only Master and Lord Jesus Christ" (v. 4, My translation).[8] This means that for Jude, the crux of their sedition is in their denial of the lordship of Jesus the Messiah. As Donald Guthrie points out, "The false teachers, whom he condemns, were those who were denying 'our only Master and Lord, Jesus Christ' (verse 1). So there is no doubt about the importance in Jude's mind of the concept of lordship."[9] And if Jesus Christ's lordship is denied, so is any supposed claim he might have on these teachers' moral allegiance. Yet if the lordship of Jesus is that important to Jude, why then does Jude seem

8. I am following the United Bible Society, Fourth Revised Edition, of this verse, because there is a small textual variant here. The Textus Receptus, upon which the Authorized Version and the New King James Version are built, takes this statement and adds *theon* after *despoten*, so that it reads like this, "the only Lord God and our Lord Jesus Christ." But the United Bible Society Fourth Revised Edition text drops *theon*, so that it draws *despoten* and *kurion* together. Now the text reads, "The only Master and Lord of us, Jesus Christ" (my translation).

9. Guthrie, *New Testament Theology*, 300.

to leave Jesus behind, not mentioning him again by name until nearly the end of this short letter, in verses 17 and 21?

Three times Jude adds a name to the title "Lord." In all three occasions (v. 4, 17, and 21) he attaches the title "Lord" to Jesus, and to ensure that there is no confusion, he then appends the title "Christ." He does not attach the title "Lord" to anyone else specifically in this letter. Therefore Jude clarifies who the Lord is throughout the letter, by defining the Lord Jesus the Messiah as the one who saved the people from out of the land of Egypt and who destroyed those who persisted in unbelief (v. 5).[10] Jude also claims that it is the Lord Jesus who reserves the rebellious angels in everlasting chains (v. 6), and he identifies the Lord Jesus as the one who will come with ten thousand holy ones to execute judgment on all (v. 14–15)[11]. Referring to verses 14–16, Duane Watson notes: "The prophecy originally referred to God's coming with an army of angels ('holy ones') in apocalyptic judgment, but by inserting the term 'Lord' (*kyrios*), Jude has made the prophecy refer to Christ's *parousia*, when he will return with his angels to execute judgment."[12]

Therefore, Jude has not left Jesus aside as marginally significant, but rather, has talked about this master and Lord throughout the whole letter, as the one whom the proto–gnostics had rejected. And what is even more noteworthy, Jude places Jesus as YHWH in the Hebrew stories. Jude obviously has a high Christology.

10. It is worth noting that the ESV follows a manuscript tradition that makes this explicit.

11. It is significant that part of the Apostolic Message regularly places Jesus at the head of the tribunal on the Day of Judgment. See for example Acts 10:36–42; 17:31; 24:24b–25.

12. Watson, "Letter of Jude," 494.

This christological hermeneutic applied to the reading of the Old Testament and telling of Israel's story is an important element in Jude, as well as in the apostolic tradition he echoes. Toward the end of *The New Testament and the People of God*, N. T. Wright makes this valuable observation:

> The worldview of the earliest Christians . . . focused on their praxis as a community, their symbols as the replacement of the Jewish symbols, and their stories as multiple, and multiform, retellings of the Jewish story. . . . It should be quite clear that what united early Christians, deeper than all the diversity, was *that they told, and lived, a form of Israel's story which reached its climax in Jesus and which then issued in their spirit-given life and task.*"[13]

The letter of Jude retells Israel's monotheistic stories, placing Jesus at the center. In this way, Jude is driving his readers toward a firmer faith, by showing that Jesus was not the messenger of some God beyond god, nor is he that demiurge who enjoys pouring out wrathful punishment in the Old Testament scriptures. Instead, Jesus and God the Father are united together in calling, loving, and preserving the faithful (v. 2, 24–25); and reserving the wicked for the Day of Judgment (v. 4, 6–7, 13–15). Jude shows us that it is not enough to simply argue for the truth, but to "portray it as it is, in all its beauty, and not neglecting its dark tones."[14] In this way, Jude defines the Jesus whom these false teachers betray.

13. Wright, *New Testament*, 456; emphasis in original.
14. Frame, *Apologetics*, 37.

REMEMBERING

Starting at verse 17, Jude urges the faithful toward specific actions, and he ends by giving them special promises. Simply put, "Jude encouraged the believers to remain firm in their faith and trust in God's promises for the future."[15] Jude's call to action admonishes believers to return to the apostolic words (v. 17), and to remember that they are experiencing nothing surprising, but those things announced by the apostles of Christ, which would come about (v. 18–19).

This recollection of apostolic teaching is stressed in 2 Peter as well, a letter that has many similarities to Jude. There, the author likewise charges believers (three times in four verses) to remember the story of Jesus (2 Pet 1:12–15). And toward the end of 2 Peter, the writer challenges them to recall the words of the prophets and the apostles (2 Pet 3:2–3), how they had rehearsed the pattern of apostasy from the past to the future. Therefore, both Jude and the author of 2 Peter encourage their people to remember the apostolic faith and the apostolic warnings. Both writers see a latent value in recalling and remembering the apostles' message.

This is the pattern that caused Martyn Lloyd-Jones to declare that the "test of Truth is its Apostolicity. Is it, and does it conform to, the apostolic message? That is the test and that is the standard."[16] This means that the apostles' message is not obsolete; it is the church's "sacred trust today."[17] Similarly it illustrates that the "words of the apostles were

---

15. Barton et al., *1 & 2 Peter* and *Jude*, 256.

16. Lloyd-Jones, *Spiritual Depression*, 183.

17. Erickson, *Christian Theology*, 1065.

already being considered authoritative and on the level with Scripture."[18]

The exhortation to remember the apostles' words and warnings fits into the charge at the beginning of Jude's letter, to contend for the faith "which was once for all delivered to the saints." Jude is able to think and talk of the faith "as a body of truths, as 'the faith' on which faith is based."[19] Jude is drawing on what the later church will call the *regula fidei* (rule of faith), which was passed on by the apostles, and which "found its expression in the canonical books of Scripture."[20]

ENVIRONMENT

Jude now describes the setting in which remembering the apostolic faith is to take place. He calls the faithful "beloved" again,[21] and then paints a picture of contrasts. Whereas the false teachers are destructive and divisive (v. 19), yet the faithful are called to be constructive (v. 20). Jude uses a present participle (*epoikodomountes*) which means *building upon something*. They are to build on the most holy faith. Though the words "your most holy faith" could be understood in a more subjective manner, yet within the context of this letter (see v. 3) Jude is driving a solid wedge between the harmful influence of the proto-gnostics and the believers' solid foundation, which is apostolic truth. Thus, "your most holy faith" is "the faith" which they have embraced as their own.

18. Barton et al., *1 & 2 Peter and Jude*, 256.
19. Jensen, *Revelation of God*, 279.
20. McGrath, *Christian Theology*, 15.
21. The first two times were in v. 1 and 3.

This idea of building on a solid foundation shows up in Paul's writings as well. In both 1 Corinthians and Ephesians, the church is viewed as a building or temple being built upon the foundation of Jesus Christ, as well as upon his apostles and prophets (1 Cor 3:9–17 and Eph 2:19–22[22]). In other words, the

> apostolic proclamation is also the foundation of the church, to which the latter has known itself to be bound from the very beginning. It is the most holy faith on which the church has to build (see Jude 20; cp. v. 17), it is the pledge transmitted to it through the apostles, the *depositum custodi* (1 Tim. 6:20; 2 Tim. 1:14; 2:2) that the church has to preserve above everything else.[23]

Jude also classifies who really has the Spirit. The errorists are the actual *psychikoi* (the soulish ones), and they do not have the Spirit (thus, they are not truly *pneumatikoi* or spiritual ones). Yet the loyal believers are privileged to pray "in the Holy Spirit." As humans live in the very oxygen they need for life, so believers live in the realm of the Spirit of God, who also breathes life into them (1 Cor 12:3 and Gal 5:16–26), and gives breath to their prayers (Rom 8:26 and Eph 6:18).

Therefore, the environment which believers inhabit in order to withstand their opponents is twofold. First, they

22. Paul inverts this order in 1 Tim 3:15, where he makes the church the pillar and ground of the truth. Might this show that in Paul's mind, there is a two-way street with regard to the truth and the church? The Scriptures form the church and call it into existence; the church supports and substantiates the Scripture in a lived–out way.

23. Ridderbos, *Redemptive History*, 15.

stand within the structure that is being built upon the most holy faith that the apostles have laid; "[Jude] pictures the faithful church as a temple where members are a holy priesthood offering spiritual sacrifices to God (Eph 2:20–22; 1 Pet 2:5)."[24] And they live within the very atmosphere of the Spirit who enlivens them and their praying. This twofold environment is found within a church milieu. It is from within the safe boundaries of the communion or fellowship that believers together remain capable of warding off the unorthodox and grow stronger in the faith.

Yet Jude has already mentioned that these false teachers had secretly entered into the fellowship (v. 4 and 12). So how can the church environment be the safe place from which believers ward off attacks? The answer to this question has two layers. First, to stay within the fellowship, and in the realm of the Word, sacraments and prayer, is to stay with Christ's people and together build, and together pray in the Spirit, and so together withstand the troublemakers. As Simon Chan argues, "Becoming a better Christian is not a matter of individual personal development. It is growing in the body with the other members."[25]

That means believers live and move within a specific praxis or behavior that is corporate and conflicts with the Gnosticism of their opponents. Watson writes, "Members of this church build up one another on faith by looking out for their spiritual welfare, in contrast to the false teachers, who divide and tear down the church."[26] This togetherness of fellowship is the very thing these subversives do not want,

24. Watson, "Letter of Jude," 497.

25. Chan, *Spiritual Theology*, 110.

26. Watson, "Letter of Jude," 497.

because it means sharing with others, it means humility, and it means living out "our common salvation" (v. 3). The opponents would rather have people following them in the "rebellion of Korah" (v. 11), as they serve only themselves (v. 12), walking "in the way of Cain" (v. 11). They would rather turn the faith in a subject-oriented direction, the individualization of the covenant, making it a "private psychological event."[27] This subject-oriented direction would, in effect, turn the fellowship into "the Church of and for the individual."[28] And a church of and for the individual is a church full of easy targets.

The second direction is more implied than specified. If the faithful are banding together in the fellowship, living within the framework that is built on the "most holy faith" and praying in the Spirit, then the day may very well come, and probably will come, when these proto-gnostics will vacate the fellowship once and for all. John mentions this when he refers to a similar group:

> Little children, it is the last hour; and as you have heard that the Antichrist is coming, even now many antichrists have come, by which we know that it is the last hour. They went out from us, but they were not of us; for if they had been of us, they would have continued with us; but they went out that they might be made manifest, that none of them were of us.[29]

27. Lee, "Protestant Gnostics," 76.
28. Ibid., 158.
29. 1 John 2:18–19

Next, it is from within the constructive environment of building upon their most holy faith, and praying in the Spirit, that believers are to keep themselves anchored in the love of God (v. 21). The word *tereo* ("to keep") is one of Jude's favorites, which he uses five times in this short letter. Its theological weight is felt in the first verse where he asserts that his readers have been preserved in Jesus Christ. There the word is a perfect, passive participle. As the Jesuit grammarian Max Zerwick notes, "the pf [perfect] envisaging the lasting result of past action."[30] Therefore, the theological significance in Jude of *tereo* seen in verse 1 is that these believers have been and are being preserved for Jesus Christ.

Concurrently, Jude also mentions in verse 1 that they are not just being preserved for Jesus Christ, but they have been and are being beloved of God.[31] Both the "keeping" and the "being loved" are the same tense in the Greek, so that, as Kelly notes, they "not only were once, but continue to be, objects of God's love and care."[32]

All of this draws us back to verse 21, where Jude charges the believers to keep themselves in the love of God. There are at least two things to notice: (1) Their preservation is in the sphere of God's love. As Leon Morris reasons, "[Jude] might have referred them to the greatness or the holiness or the majesty of God. But when he selects one quality to characterize Deity, it is love"[33]; (2) Jude is not telling them

30. Zerwick, *Grammatical Analysis*, 738.

31. I am again following the UBS Fourth Rev. Ed. The Textus Receptus reads "sanctified."

32. Kelly, *Peter and Jude*, 243

33. Morris, *Testaments of Love*, 140.

to earn that love. Instead, the command of verse 21 ("keep yourselves") is grounded in the declaration of verse 1 ("To those who are . . . preserved in Jesus Christ"). And so they must continue to remind themselves of what is already true and allow that to steer them and shore up their fidelity. "The writer's implied point is that as Christians his readers are the objects of God's love, but through backsliding or infidelity they can lose their awareness of it or erect barriers between themselves and it."[34]

Yet this keeping of themselves in the love of God ought to spread out into their response toward one another. Tokunboh Adeyemo describes how this should flesh itself out in the fellowship:

> The distinguishing mark of Christ's disciples is love (John 13:35). We are first brought into God's family by his love [Jude 1]. Now Jude says, *keep yourselves in God's love as you wait* (21). Love to care for one another, love to support one another, love to correct one another, and love to speak the truth to one another (Eph 4:25).[35]

Along with the command to keep themselves in the love of God, Jude adds a present participle: *prosdexomenoi*. This participle appears to be attendant with the main verb, *tereo*. While *keeping* themselves in the love of God (looking backward and at the present), they are to *be watching with eager anticipation* for the mercy of our Lord Jesus Christ with the goal of eternal life (looking forward). Jude's point is that they are not only to dwell on what has been accom-

---

34. Kelly, *Peter and Jude*, 286.

35. Adeyemo, "Jude," 1568.

plished for them in the past and to keep living in its present truth; they are to look forward to the day of Christ's vindicating return. At that moment they will be openly affirmed and vindicated by Christ as God's own children, and heirs of the mercy of God and the life of God. In the words of the "Westminster Shorter Catechism," "At the resurrection, believers . . . shall be openly acknowledged and acquitted in the day of judgement."[36]

Therefore, in remembering the words of the apostles of Christ (v. 17) and remembering what God has done for them in Christ (v. 21a) and what they can expectantly look forward to at Christ's return (v. 21b), believers are then to be God's means of grace to those who are being led away by the troublemakers (v. 22–23).

THOSE STRAYING

Though there are significant textual variations in verses 22 and 23, it is nevertheless obvious that Jude is addressing the fact that Christians are not to be in self-preservation mode. Rather they must take risks for the sake of restraining those who have begun to be infected by the false teachers and their false teaching, and restoring those who have fallen into their destructive clutches: "We should have contact without contamination."[37] This is an interesting turn in Jude's directives. Though keeping oneself from the infections of the proto-gnostics is important to Jude, yet it must not end there. If judgment is going to fall on these disobedient ones as it fell on the rebels aligned with Korah (v. 11), then the

36. "Westminster Shorter Catechism," 39.
37. Adeyemo, "Jude," 1568.

aim is to "speak to the congregation, saying, 'Get away from the tents of Korah, Dathan, and Abiram.' . . . Touch nothing of theirs, lest you be consumed in all their sins."[38]

COMFORTING PROMISES

Finally, Jude ends with promises that echo what he had declared back in verse 1. God is the one able to keep the faithful, to sustain them, and to present them blameless before his presence on the Day of Christ. Now sing for joy and be in grateful awe of God (v. 24–25). The value of these final two verses has to do with the God-centeredness of the most holy faith. It is God who keeps (*tereo*) his people from crashing headlong into perdition. It is God who presents the believers spotless and clean before his own presence with great joy. And it is the only God our Savior who does this, through Jesus Christ our Lord, to whom belong honor and glory, dominion and power endlessly. Watson states it clearly: "The doxology attributes our salvation as a people of God completely to God."[39]

CONCLUSION

Jude's primary way forward in contending for the faith is: Remember!

1. Remember the faith once for all delivered to the saints.

2. Remember the faith taught through the apostles.

---

38. Num 16:24, 26b.
39. Watson, "Letter of Jude," 500.

3. Remember that our master and Lord, Jesus the Messiah of history and faith, is in the place of YHWH in Israel's stories.[40]

4. Remember that God the Father and our master and Lord, Jesus Christ, have called, loved, and preserved you.

5. Remember the great love of God in Jesus Christ for you.

6. Remember that Jesus is coming again and will vindicate you with the mercy and life of God.

7. Remember that our Lord Jesus is coming with tens of thousands of his holy ones to judge the traitorous.

8. Do this remembering within the ecclesial context of word, sacraments, and prayer.[41]

9. Remember that this contending for the faith should be salvific for others as well, a means of rescuing those who are too close to the place where God's judgment may soon break out.

This assessment from Jude is important for building a strong faith in a congregation that affirms that the Holy Scripture is inspired by God "to be the rule of faith and life."[42] And a strong faith will deprive modern Gnosticism of its power to harm. Remember!

---

40. Wright, *Last Word*, 50.
41. Hart, *Deconstructing Evangelicalism*, 117.
42. "Westminster Confession of Faith," I.2.

4

Historical Theology

*"Salvation then, according to the Bible, is not
something that was discovered, but something that
happened. . . . For Christian experience depends
absolutely upon an event."*[1]

*"The goal of the Spirit is transformation into the im-
age of God as that is expressed in Christ's humanity,
so that believers become progressively more truly and
fully human."*[2]

*"Once sin has been overcome and man's harmony
with God restored, creation is reconciled, too."*[3]

SEVERAL DECADES after Jude had written his letter, another church leader, Irenaeus, arose who was alarmed
by what he saw in a group of people whom he called
"Gnostics." To rebut the renegade group, he wrote a five-
volume work, which he titled, *A Refutation and Subversion*

1. Machen, *Christianity and Liberalism*, 70–1.
2. Ferguson, *Holy Spirit*, 112–13.
3. Benedict, *Jesus of Nazareth*, 27.

of Knowledge Falsely So Called.[4] In this chapter, I explain in brief the format of Irenaeus's five-volume work, and will, in a few words, discuss the continued impact he has with modern gnostics. Next, I will show what his major focus was and why he took this approach. Finally, I will draw from his arguments those points that are important in withstanding the modern gnostics.

THE FIVE BOOKS OF IRENAEUS

In his first book, Irenaeus spends a large portion of his time explaining the complex and highly technical system of gnostic dogmas. He recognizes that Gnosticism is not a monolithic program, but a series of Gnosticisms, where each teacher breeds his own brand and version: "We have judged it well to point out, first of all, in what respects the very fathers of this fable differ among themselves, as if they were inspired by different spirits of error."[5] He then traces the genealogy of gnostic heresy back to Simon Magus. In book two, he demonstrates the inconsistencies of the gnostic systems, providing rational "proofs that their doctrines are false."[6] Finally, in books three through five Irenaeus works out evidences and arguments from the Scriptures and the apostles' Gospel declaration with regard to God, and his Son Jesus Christ, who is the truth and no lie. John

4. This work is often titled, *Against Heresies*. For brevity's sake, I will so call it throughout this chapter. Though Irenaeus wrote his books in Greek, they have survived mainly in Latin. There are Greek fragments which still remain; the most important are found in Eusebius and Epiphanius (Grant, *Irenaeus*, 6).

5. Irenaeus, *Against Heresies*, 330; I.IX.5.

6. Grant, *Irenaeus*, 6.

Behr captures the direction of books three through five as he describes their main points in the introduction to his translation of another of Irenaeus's works, *On Apostolic Preaching*: "He then skillfully interweaves passages from the Old Testament and the New, to demonstrate that there is but one God, who has made Himself known in His one Son, Jesus Christ, through the one Holy Spirit, to the one human race, through the one all-encompassing divine economy or history."[7]

IRENAEUS'S EFFECTIVENESS

To gauge the effectiveness of Irenaeus's approach in his day would be hard to do on a quantitative level, though it does appear that the "foes of Egyptian Gnosticism early found it helpful. Clement soon used it in Alexandria, Tertullian in Carthage, Hippolytus in Rome."[8] Yet one way to judge his present-day effectiveness is to observe that those who see themselves as modern gnostics still interact with Irenaeus. They may do so by describing his work and then dismissing it as a piece of polemical propaganda, as Karen King does when she describes Irenaeus's work as a strategy "to construct heresy."[9] Or they may do so by describing his work, wrestling with it, and attempting to refute his arguments. In this way they admit that, "Irenaeus's characterization, however hostile, nevertheless is accurate."[10] The point is that after 1,800 years, Irenaeus still evokes fairly serious re-

---

7. Behr, "Demonstration," 15.

8. Grant, *Irenaeus*, 7.

9. King, *Gnosticism*, 2–3.

10. Pagels, *Beyond Belief*, 138.

sponses from gnostics.[11] This shows that he continues to be an ally for those who desire to refute Gnosticism's various forms in each age.

IRENAEUS'S MAJOR FOCUS:
THEOLOGY AND THEOGONY

The Gnosticism of Irenaeus's day presented a diverse structure of religious theory and pious talk. "They knew something of Greek philosophy, more about theosophy, and their fondness for dualistic thought, speculative cosmology, mythology, and spiritualizing ideas about Christ, all expressed in mysterious language, won them some converts."[12] As N. T. Wright has poignantly observed, "the Gnostics were the cultural conservatives, sticking with the kind of religion that everyone already knew."[13]

Because of the diversity, Irenaeus and other early church apologists had to know their subject and grasp the core ideas of Gnosticism. Philip Jenkins describes the accuracy of the early apologists, including Irenaeus, this way:

> While these writings made no pretense at objectivity, they were richly informative about the core ideas of the various movements, and as more heretical texts have been found, we can

---

11. From a glance at the indices of Pagels's main works (for example, *Adam, Eve, and the Serpent*; *The Gnostic Gospels*; *Beyond Belief*; and *The Origin of Satan*), the reader can see she mentions Irenaeus more often than any other author or human figure, with the exception of Jesus. Also, it is worthwhile to notice that Hans Jonas gives Irenaeus at least as much space as he does Plato, Plotinus, and Theodore bar Konai.

12. Grant, *Irenaeus*, 11.

13. Wright, *Gospel of Jesus*, 101.

> see that the Fathers were quoting their enemies'
> opinions quite fully and accurately. Partly, the
> Fathers were demonstrating a sense of fairness
> by quoting their enemies objectively, but in ad-
> dition, orthodox writers plausibly felt that the
> views they were quoting were so contorted and
> ludicrous that the heretics were best condemned
> out of their own mouths.[14]

Because Irenaeus knew his gnostic opponents so well, he focused on areas where they needed to be refuted in his day. Those areas were primarily theology proper and theogony.[15] Irenaeus also focused on other issues, but the study of the One God and a refutation of the gnostic systems of spawned aeons, the demiurge, and the fragmented pleroma are regularly repeated themes, most pointedly in the first two books while being woven into the remaining three books as well. Eric Osborn observes that evidence of the strength of Irenaeus's mind "and strong digestive system," which enabled him to "handle the tedious monstrosities of the heretics,"[16] are found in the early pages of his first book.

IRENAEUS'S HELPFUL CHRISTOLOGY

In addition to theology and theogony, Irenaeus vigorously focused his efforts on Christology. W. H. C. Frend describes the various threads of Irenaeus's christological themes, then notes, "To Irenaeus, however, belongs the credit of

14. Jenkins, *Hidden Gospels*, 29.

15. By "theogony" I mean the birth, formation, and genealogy of God, the aeons, and the demiurge.

16. Osborn, *Irenaeus*, 7.

systematizing these ideas and welding them into a coherent theology."[17]

I will present some of Irenaeus's primary aspects of Christology, and what it is that ties them together "into a coherent theology." Throughout I will point to ways that this Irenaean Christology is supremely useful in contending for the faith once for all delivered to the saints.[18] The reason for focusing more on Irenaeus's christological answer to Gnosticism, rather than his response to their misplaced theology and hierarchy of powers, is that the twenty-first century struggle in our congregations is not likely to be over the latter. Instead it seems to me that the present fight is in the area of Christology and some of the collateral consequences of that Christology.

The Word of God: This Flesh-and-Blood Man

Irenaeus assumed a singular God who was the God of the Hebrew Scriptures, behind whom there was no other god: "The rule of truth which we hold, is, that there is one God Almighty, who made all things by His Word, and fashioned and formed, out of that which had no existence, all things which exist."[19] Again, Irenaeus states even more fully:

> It is proper, then, that I should begin with the first and most important head, that is, God the Creator, who made the heaven and the earth, and all things that are therein (whom these men blasphemously style the fruit of a defect),

17. Frend, *Rise*, 248.
18. Jude 3.
19. Irenaeus, *Against Heresies*, 347; I.XXII.1.

and to demonstrate that there is nothing either
above Him or after Him; nor that, influenced by
any one, but of His own free will, He created all
things, since He is the only God, the only Lord,
the only Creator, the only Father, alone contain-
ing all things, and Himself commanding all
things into existence.[20]

While maintaining this monotheism, Irenaeus posits
that the sole God has, as it were, two hands, and these two
hands are the Son and the Spirit: "Now man is a mixed
organization of soul and flesh, who was formed after the
likeness of God, and moulded by His hands, that is, by the
Son and Holy Spirit, to whom also He said, 'Let Us make
man.'"[21] Though the picture is metaphorical and anthropo-
morphic, nevertheless Irenaeus gets across to his readers
the point that the only God and His Son and Spirit have
existed simultaneously. For in Irenaeus's thinking, there is
"simultaneity of the begetting and the procession of the Son
and of the Spirit" expressed in this picture of "two hands."
And this image "excludes any chronological or conceptual

20. Ibid., 359; II.I.1. In another place, Irenaeus wrote, "Such, then,
are the first principles of the Gospel: that there is one God, the Maker
of this universe; He who was also announced by the prophets, and
who by Moses set forth the dispensation of the law, [principles] which
proclaim the Father of our Lord Jesus Christ, and ignore any other
God or Father except Him" (428; III.XI.7).

21. Ibid., 463; IV.Preface.4. Also: "For by the hands of the Father,
that is, by the Son and the Holy Spirit, man, and not merely a part of
man, was made in the likeness of God." And again, "moulded at the
beginning by the hands of God, that is, of the Son and of the Spirit"
(531 and 557; V.VI.1 and XXVIII.4).

anteriority of the begetting of the Son to the procession of the Spirit."[22]

The existence of the Father with the Son and the Spirit is durative: "For with Him were always present the Word and Wisdom, the Son and the Spirit, by whom and in whom, freely and spontaneously, He made all things, to whom also He speaks, saying, 'Let Us make man after Our image and likeness.'"[23] In another place he specifically refers to the Son, saying, "But the Son, eternally co-existing with the Father, from of old."[24]

Irenaeus affirms repeatedly the ontological identity of the Father and the Son. [25] For example, he states: "Christ Himself, therefore, together with the Father, is God of the living, who spake to Moses, and who was also manifested to the fathers."[26] And then, just a few paragraphs later, he announces: "And through the Word Himself who had been made visible and palpable, was the Father shown forth, although all did not equally believe in Him; but all saw the Father in the Son: for the Father is the invisible of the Son, but the Son the visible of the Father."[27]

According to Irenaeus, then, Christ the Son and Word of God is not only simultaneous with the Father, but He

22. Bobrinskoy, *Mystery*, 286.

23. Irenaeus, *Against Heresies*, 487;V.XX.1.

24. Ibid., 406; II.XXX.9.

25. *Ontological identity* has to do with the fact that the Father, the Son, and the Holy Spirit are "the same in substance, equal in power and glory" ("Westminster Shorter Catechism," 6). See also the Nicene Creed.

26. Irenaeus, *Against Heresies*, 467; IV.V.2.

27. Ibid., 469; IV.VI.6.

and the Father make up the being known as God.[28] Irenaeus also rehearses what the Church believes specifically about Christ Jesus: "Christ Jesus, our Lord, and God, and Saviour, and King."[29]

From these statements, it is clear that Irenaeus not only affirms the divinity of Christ Jesus, but is affirming the Trinity (though this idea is not highly developed), where there is:

> but one living and true God, everlasting, without body, parts, or passions; of infinite power, wisdom, and goodness; the maker and preserver of all things both visible and invisible. And in unity of this Godhead there be three Persons, of one substance, power, and eternity; the Father, the Son, and the Holy Ghost.[30]

But where might we come to meet and know this Christ? As already stated, in Jesus:

> For Christ did not at that time descend upon Jesus, neither was Christ one and Jesus another: but the Word of God—who is the Saviour of all, and the ruler of heaven and earth, who is Jesus, as I have already pointed out, who did also take upon Him flesh, and was anointed by the Spirit from the Father—was made Jesus Christ.[31]

The importance of this statement should be clear. The gnostics "utter blasphemy, also, against our Lord," placing

28. This does not exclude the Spirit's place. See what has already been cited about the two hands of God.

29. Ibid., 330; I.X.1.

30. *Book of Common Prayer*, "Articles of Religion," Article 1.

31. Irenaeus, *Against Heresies*, 423; III.IX.3.

a wedge between the historical Jesus and the divine Christ, "by cutting off and dividing Jesus from Christ."[32] Their anticosmic dualism forced them to bypass the historical Jesus to grasp for the Christ who is beyond flesh and blood. "To *know* Christ was not in any sense to have knowledge about the 'historical man of flesh and blood' but rather to be personally related to the mystical heavenly being who liberates humanity from historical concerns."[33]

This dividing the Jesus of history from the Christ of faith follows a platonic pattern. As C. C. Taylor notes in his forward to Plato's *Protagoras*, as Plato records Socrates's supposed dialogue with Protagoras, "What is crucial is that, for Plato's apologetic and philosophical purposes, historical truth is largely irrelevant."[34] Even one of novelist P. D. James's clerical characters falls into this splitting up the historical Jesus from the living Christ, thus making the historical irrelevant. Inspector Dalgliesh asks Father Martin, If it could be proved Jesus never physically (thus historically) was raised from the dead, would that make a difference to his faith? Father Martin responds in a way that might make any gnostic smile, "My son, for one who every hour of his life has the assurance of the living presence of Christ, why should I worry about what happened to earthly bones?"[35]

But Irenaeus's point is that to partition off the Jesus of history from the Christ of faith is to keep God far away

32. Ibid., IV.Preface.3.

33. Lee, *Protestant Gnostics*, 20.

34. Plato and Taylor, *Protagoras*, xiv.

35. James, *Holy Orders*, 275. I'm not claiming that P. D. James is a gnostic. But her clerical character, Fr. Martin, announces almost verbatim what I have heard clergy and laypeople say in the past.

from our creaturely condition, with all of its suffering, grief, and fallenness. Therefore, as Irenaeus perceives, atoning reconciliation between God and man

> had to be regarded as including the whole of our Lord's incarnate life from his cradle to his grave in which, as one of us and one with us, he shared all our experiences, overcoming our disobedience through his obedience and sanctifying every stage of human life, and thereby vivified and restored our humanity to communion with God.[36]

In other words, if we would meet God, we must meet him in the Word made man, Jesus of Nazareth, the flesh-and-blood man. This is what von Balthasar addresses in a lengthy statement that deserves to be quoted in full:

> In contrast to the Gnostics' empty spiritualism and proud contempt for the body, [Irenaeus] stubbornly refuses to let man cut himself off from the life of this world and escape into a pseudo-heavenly half-existence. Irenaeus is the outspoken champion of the 'realism' of Christian theology. If there is to be a real redemption, this earth and no other, this body and no other, must have the capacity to take God's grace to itself.
>
> At the centre . . . is the image of the Son of Man, who unites heaven and earth. He is the first touch-stone of Christian truth. Only in Him is there resolution of the paradox which Gnosticism tried in vain to master: God by nature is invisible, yet man by nature desires the vision of God.

---

36. Torrance, *Trinitarian Faith*, 166–67.

But this uniting of God and world takes place
in the Passion of Christ, when He is stretched out
between height and depth, breadth and length.
The cross-beams are the world's true centre.[37]

Though Irenaeus does not use the technical terminology of the "hypostatic union" of the two natures of Christ, yet in the second century he is already affirming much of what will be hammered out in the fourth century in the Council of Nicea and the later Nicene Creed.

Irenaeus's second-century claims, therefore, do not fit the fantastic assertion made by one of Dan Brown's characters in *The Da Vinci Code*:

"My dear," Teabing declared, "until *that* moment in history, Jesus was viewed by his followers as a mortal prophet . . . a great and powerful man, but a *man* nonetheless. A mortal." [38]

"Not the Son of God?"

"Right," Teabing said, "Jesus' establishment as 'the Son of God' was officially proposed and voted on by the Council of Nicea."

"Hold on. You're saying Jesus' divinity was the result of a *vote*?"

"A relatively close vote at that," Teabing added.[39]

From Irenaeus we learn the importance of affirming:

1. There is only one God, the God of Abraham, Isaac and Jacob (monotheism).

37. Irenaeus and Balthasar, *Scandal*, 13.
38. Teabing is referring to the Council of Nicea in 325 A.D. 325.
39. Brown, *Da Vinci Code*, 233.

2. This one God is simultaneously three persons: the Father, Son, and Holy Spirit (trinitarianism).

3. We come to meet this one God in the flesh-and-blood man, Jesus Christ.

4. We don't divide what God has put together, the Jesus of history and the Christ of faith.

5. Time and space history is the field on which God plays out His world-rescue operation.

In the Scripture

Irenaeus is also adamant that we come to meet this God and his Word by means of the Hebrew Scriptures:

> But as we follow for our teacher the one and only true God, and possess His words as the rule of truth, we do all speak alike with regard to the same things, knowing but one God, the Creator of this universe, who sent the prophets, who led forth the people from the land of Egypt, who in these last times manifested His own Son, that He might put the unbelievers to confusion, and search out the fruit of righteousness.[40]

As Osborn notes, "Irenaeus knows of no other proof which can stand beside the testimony of Scripture."[41] That Scripture testimony is also the story of Israel, climaxing in Jesus Christ. This is one of the points Behr makes when he writes, "Put in another way, the canon of truth is the formal structure of the harmony of [Old Testament] scripture, read

40. Irenaeus, *Against Heresies*, 439; IV.XXXV.4.
41. Osborn, *Irenaeus*, 171.

as speaking of the Christ revealed in the apostolic preaching 'in accordance with the scripture.'"[42] It is this christocentric texture of Scripture that leads Irenaeus to claim, "the writings of Moses are the words of Christ." And not only Moses, but "beyond doubt, the words of the other prophets are His [words], as I have pointed out."[43]

The revealing of God and his Word is passed on as well in the apostolic tradition: "The Church, though dispersed throughout the whole world, even to the ends of the earth, has received from the apostles and their disciples this faith."[44] This tradition passed on by the apostles found its expression in the canonical books of Christian Scriptures.[45] Along these same lines N. T. Wright observes, "Paul is most conscious that he is writing as one authorized, by the apostolic call he had received from Jesus Christ, and in the power of the Spirit, to bring life and order to the church by his words."[46] Wright further affirms that Paul was not the only apostolic writer to perceive his vocation in this manner. That the writers of the New Testament "were conscious of a unique vocation to write Jesus-shaped, Spirit-led, church-shaping books, as part of their strange first-generation calling, we should not doubt."[47]

Irenaeus goes on to claim that this apostolic tradition is pointedly handed down in the canonical Gospels. As he says with regard to the Gospel according to Luke,

---

42. Behr, *Mystery*, 61.

43. Irenaeus, *Against Heresies*, 464; IV.II.3.

44. Ibid., 330; I.X.1.

45. McGrath, *Christian Theology*, 15.

46. Wright, *Last Word*, 51.

47. Ibid., 52.

> God set forth very many Gospel truths, through
> Luke's instrumentality, which all should esteem
> it necessary to use, in order that all persons, fol-
> lowing his subsequent testimony, which treats
> upon the acts and the doctrine of the apostles,
> and holding the unadulterated rule of truth, may
> be saved. His testimony, therefore, is true, and
> the doctrine of the apostles is open and steadfast,
> holding nothing in reserve; nor did they teach
> one set of doctrines in private, and another in
> public.[48]

Therefore, with regard to the four Gospels, "Irenaeus
does not create the situation of a closed canon for the
Gospels, rather he recognizes it, and attempts to give some
significance to it."[49] And what is it that sets the canonical
Gospels apart from the later writings of the gnostics? Each
of the "Gospels of Matthew, Mark, Luke and John are centered upon the Passion of Christ and are proclaimed using
the treasury of the scripture, the Old Testament."[50] By contrast, the noncanonical "Gospels," like *The Gospel of Thomas*
or the Valentinian *Gospel of Truth*, are either empty of the
apostolic shape which centered on the passion of Christ
"according to the Scriptures," or approach Christ and the
Scriptures with a "whole new scheme of salvation through
knowledge, and an unknowable father in the heavenly
realm of light, which is the pleroma or fullness."[51]

48. Irenaeus, *Against Heresies*, 439; III.XV.1.

49. Behr, "Demonstration," 15 fn 6.

50. Behr, *Mystery*, 62.

51. Barnstone and Meyer, *Gnostic Bible*, 240.

Therefore Irenaeus robustly blends together with the Hebrew Scriptures the apostolic tradition as the means by which humans may come to meet and know this God and his Word. "The great achievement of Irenaeus is twofold: he organised the structure of scripture and he set out the apostolic tradition using both the sayings of the lord and the writings which were canonised."[52]

From Irenaeus we learn that as Christians it is important to affirm:

1. That we meet Jesus, the Word and Son of God, in the Hebrew Scriptures (Old Testament);

2. That the words of Moses and the Prophets are to be heard as the words spoken by Jesus;

3. That the apostles of Christ passed on the truth of Christ Jesus in the Gospels and in their writings (the apostolic tradition);

4. That the apostolic pattern of sound words is centered on the passion of Christ and gladly uses the treasury of the Old Testament.

Creation

If the Word of God, who is one with the Father and the Spirit, is met in the flesh-and-blood man Jesus Christ, then creation is in some way part of God's world-liberation program. Irenaeus addresses this, while placing Christ the Savior at the center:

52. Osborn, *Irenaeus*, 182.

> God having predestined that the first man
> should be of an animal nature, with this view,
> that he might be saved by the spiritual one. For
> inasmuch as He had a pre-existence as a saving
> Being, it was necessary that what might be saved
> should also be called into existence in order that
> the Being who saves should not exist in vain.[53]

This statement raises a few questions. If God created
in order to bring about salvation and to be known as Savior,
does that make God the originator of sin and the destructive consequences of the fall? Based on the whole body of
Against Heretics, that doesn't seem to be what Irenaeus is affirming. Instead, as Behr notes, Irenaeus can say this only by
looking backward at creation through the incarnation and
crucifixion of the Word of God: "the solution comes first,
and then we begin to understand where the problem lies.
Christ is . . . the first principle or hypothesis for all Christian
theology."[54] In other words, history is read retrospectively
through the lens of the incarnation, crucifixion, and resurrection of Jesus Christ. For example, "theology moves from
the historical statement, that Jesus Christ was put to death,
to the theological affirmation that he gave himself up for
the life of the world."[55] This means that salvation history,
per se, "is written from the perspective of the Cross, with its
totality—creation, human sinfulness, the giving of the law,
the preparation, and the work of salvation—simultaneously

---

53. Irenaeus, *Against Heresies*, 455;III.XXII.3.

54. Behr, *Mystery*, 84.

55. Ibid.

revealed in and through the proclamation of the crucified and risen Christ, the eternal plan or economy of God."[56]

Christ, then, provides the "diagnosis of our condition and simultaneously provides the remedy."[57] That is why, as Lesslie Newbigin reminds us, "we have to read the whole story from Genesis onward as having its true interpretation in the total fact of the incarnation—the birth, ministry, death, resurrection, and glory of Jesus."[58] Or, to put in a different way, "We do not argue from experience to the gospel. On the contrary, it is the gospel accepted in faith which enables us to experience all reality in a new way and to find that all reality does indeed reflect the glory of God."[59]

Therefore, creation and the history, or multiple histories, of the world, "when viewed from the encounter with Christ, are known as having been always guided by his providence in such a way that it finds its source and fulfillment in him."[60] And from the place of the "once for all" work of Christ, creation and its history look backward and forward and see "everything in this light, making everything new."[61] The cross is impregnated "in the very structure of creation: *stat crux dum volvitur orbis*—the Cross stands, while the earth revolves."[62] This reading creation and creation's history through the cross

56. Ibid., 88.
57. Ibid., 92.
58. Newbigin, *Proper Confidence*, 89.
59. Ibid., 96–97.
60. Behr, *Mystery*, 89.
61. Ibid., 90.
62. Ibid.

is echoed in Martin Luther: "The cross, said Luther, is the test of everything (*Crux probat omnia*)."[63]

Irenaeus thus refutes gnostic anticosmic dualism. Creation is not the consequence of a fall, but is part of the eternal design of God, his design of salvation and restoration. This can only be seen through the passion of Christ, from incarnation to coronation. From this new way of seeing things, of telling the world's story, we find that creation is good, the fall was somehow part of the mystery, and the redemption and liberation of humankind and creation in Christ is the climax.[64] Therefore, instead of needing to escape a creation that is bad to the bone, we long for restoration. "Now this is His Word, our Lord Jesus Christ, who in the last times was made a man among men, that He might join the end to the beginning, that is, man to God."[65]

In Christ's passion, in which grace restores and transforms nature, we will find that the fall was an essential part, providentially, for humankind's good:

> This, therefore, was the [object of the] long-suffering of God, that man, passing through all things, and acquiring the knowledge of moral discipline, then attaining to the resurrection from the dead, and learning by experience what is the source of his deliverance, may always live in a state of gratitude to the Lord, having obtained from Him the gift of incorruptibility, that he might love Him the more.[66]

---

63. Macleod, *From Glory*, 86.

64. Wright, *Paul*, 21–39.

65. Irenaeus, *Against Heresies*, 488; IV.XX.4.

66. Ibid., 450; III.XX.2. Irenaeus makes much of the place of death

At this point it might be helpful to restate the main thrust of this section before moving to the next. Irenaeus's assertion about the reason and purpose of creation (and so history, humanity, etc.) are summed up in these words: "For inasmuch as He had a pre-existence as a saving Being, it was necessary that what might be saved should also be called into existence in order that the Being who saves should not exist in vain."[67] Therefore creation was for Christ, the Word of God, to become man, and bring about our restoration;

> but when He became incarnate, and was made man, He commenced afresh the long line of human beings, and furnished us, in a brief, comprehensive manner, with salvation; so that what we had lost in Adam—namely, to be according to the image and likeness of God—we might recover in Christ Jesus.[68]

Irenaeus teaches us that the Christian can, and ought to, gladly affirm the following:

1. Creation, along with all creatures, was created good, and God has never despised it;

2. Creation is part of God's plan;

3. Creation and its history are read through the lens of the incarnation, crucifixion, and resurrection of Christ Jesus;

4. Christ provides the diagnosis and the remedy for our condition;

in this regard: 449–50; III.XX.1.

67. Ibid., 455; III.XXII.3.

68. Ibid., 446; III.XVIII.1.

5. Creation and history are guided by Christ's providential hand in a way that shows their source and fulfillment are in him;

6. Grace, therefore, restores, fulfills, and renews nature.

Incarnation, Recapitulation, and Restoration

Yet how can we recover what was lost in Adam? Irenaeus begins to answer this question by stating the reason why Jesus had to be God and man:

> Therefore, as I have already said, He caused man (human nature) to cleave to and to become, one with God. For unless man had overcome the enemy of man, the enemy would not have been legitimately vanquished. And again: unless it had been God who had freely given salvation, we could never have possessed it securely. And unless man had been joined to God, he could never have become a partaker of incorruptibility. For it was incumbent upon the Mediator between God and men, by His relationship to both, to bring both to friendship and concord, and present man to God, while He revealed God to man. For, in what way could we be partakers of the adoption of sons, unless we had received from Him through the Son that fellowship which refers to Himself, unless His Word, having been made flesh, had entered into communion with us?[69]

69. Ibid., 448; II.XVIII.7. See also: 449; III.XIX.3 and 545; V.XVII.3.

For the Word of God to be our Savior, he must then be God and man, "in two distinct natures, but one person forever."[70] Irenaeus's logic pressed up hard against the gnostics' because their Christ did not need to be God and man, since their God did not desire to save the creation, and specifically our humanity, body and soul. But in Irenaeus's statement, he shows that Jesus the Christ, man cleaving to God and one with God, was capable of bringing about a full-bodied fellowship and reconciliation between the One God and humankind. In Hans Boersma's words, "Irenaeus is consistently and strongly antidocetic."[71]

Irenaeus carries this theme a bit further when he promotes the argument that for the Word of God to destroy sin and its effects, he must become as fully human as those who are drawn by sin into bondage:

> For it behoved Him who was to destroy sin, and redeem man under the power of death, that He should Himself be made that very same thing which he was, that is, man; who had been drawn by sin into bondage, but was held by death, so that sin should be destroyed by man, and man should go forth from death. For as by the disobedience of the one man who was originally moulded from virgin soil, the many were made sinners, and forfeited life; so was it necessary that, by the obedience of one man, who was originally born from a virgin, many should be justified and receive salvation. Thus, then, was the Word of God made man, as also Moses says: "God, true are His

70. "Westminster Shorter Catechism," 21.

71. Boersma, *Violence*, 122. *Docetism* was the ancient heresy that claimed Jesus was so fully God that he only appeared to be human. Thus *antidocetic* is the complete opposite of Docetism.

works." But if, not having been made flesh, He did appear as if flesh, His work was not a true one. But what He did appear, that He also was: God recapitulated in Himself the ancient formation of man, that He might kill sin, deprive death of its power, and vivify man; and therefore His works are true.[72]

Here Irenaeus puts forward a case that sounds much like Gregory of Nazianzus, who some years later stated, "For that which he [Christ] has not assumed he has not healed; but that which is united to his Godhead is also saved."[73] Thus, Irenaeus doesn't limit salvation to one aspect of humanity, but to the whole of our humanness. It is a full salvation because the Christian God made the whole human being. And because the whole human being has now fallen, God must become so fully human that it can be said, "God has fully saved His creature."[74]

Irenaeus then pulls together the themes of creation, fall, incarnation, and redemptive atonement by affirming that Christ recapitulated in his life, death, and resurrection the Adamic predicament. As Boersma notes, "The theory of recapitulation clearly implies that it is not only the death of Christ but also the life of Christ that has redemptive value."[75]

This recapitulation comes out at different levels. For example, as Adam was molded out of virgin soil, Christ was "originally born from a virgin."[76] As by Adam's dis-

72. Irenaeus, *Against Heresies*, 448; II.XVIII.7.

73. Nazianzus, "To Cledonius," 218.

74. See Nazianzus, 218.

75. Boersma, *Violence*, 124.

76. Irenaeus, *Against Heresies*, 448; III.XVIII.7. This is referred to

obedience many were made sinners and forfeited life, so by Christ's own obedience "many should be justified and receive salvation."[77] As Adam's disobedience came by a tree, so Christ cancels it out at a tree:

> For doing away with [the effects of] that dis-
> obedience of man which had taken place at the
> beginning by the occasion of a tree, "He became
> obedient unto death, even the death of the cross;"
> rectifying that disobedience which had occurred
> by reason of a tree, through that obedience which
> was [wrought out] upon the tree [of the cross].[78]

Therefore, by this action he brought us back into friendship with God by means of his incarnation, "propitiating indeed for us the Father against whom we had sinned, and cancelling (*consolatus*) our disobedience by His own obedience; conferring also upon us the gift of communion with, and subjection to, our Maker."[79] Boersma calls attention to this exchange of Christ's obedience in place of Adam's disobedience, focusing on Christ's temptations; "He includes all humanity in his person, so that when he overcomes the temptation of sin, humanity—at least in principle—has overcome the temptation of sin."[80]

repeatedly by Irenaeus. For example, see III.XXI.10 and also chapter XXII.4.

77. Irenaeus, *Against Heresies*, 448.II.XVIII.7. See also: "For as by one man's disobedience sin entered, and death obtained [a place] through sin; so also by the obedience of one man, righteousness having been introduced, shall cause life to fructify in those persons who in times past were dead" (454; III.XXI.10).

78. Irenaeus, *Against Heresies*, 544; V.XVI.3.

79. Ibid., 544; V.XVII.1.

80. Ibid., 126.

For the gnostic, however, "the fundamental problem in human life is not sin but ignorance, and the best way to address this problem is not through faith but through knowledge."[81] That means escape from the alienation of creation is paramount, along with gaining the "knowledge of God and the essential oneness of the self with God."[82] The gnostic would be able to give her assent to William Willimon's rather tongue-in-cheek statement, "Unable to preach Christ and him crucified, we preach humanity and it improved."[83] For the gnostic, restoration by means of Christ's incarnation is not essential, overcoming sin is not important, and undoing Adam's disobedience by Christ's obedience is not necessary. Simply to escape from creation by means of gnosis is what the gnostic desires. But for Irenaeus, and the faithful whom he represents, the restoration of humankind, body and soul, through the recapitulating action of Christ, is the singular means by which humanity has any hope of salvation.

Likewise, through this recapitulation, we also find release from our debts, so that as "by means of a tree we were made debtors to God, [so also] by means of a tree we may obtain the remission of our debt."[84] By recapitulating our humanness in Himself, Christ sought "to kill sin, deprive death of its power, . . . vivify man,"[85] undo our disobedience with his obedience, restore fellowship with God, wage war "against our enemy . . . crushing him who had at the begin-

81. Meyer, "Introduction," 7.

82. Ibid., 5.

83. Willimon, *Peculiar Speech*, 9.

84. Irenaeus, *Against Heresies*, 545; V.XVII.3.

85. Ibid., 448; III.XVIII.7.

ning led us away captives in Adam, and [trampling] upon his head,"[86] and bring man into the adoption of sons:

> For it was for this end that the Word of God was made man, and He who was the Son of God became the Son of man, that man, having been taken into the Word, and receiving the adoption, might become the son of God. For by no other means could we have attained to incorruptibility and immortality, unless we had been united to incorruptibility and immortality. But how could we be joined to incorruptibility and immortality, unless, first, incorruptibility and immortality had become that which we also are, so that the corruptible might be swallowed up by incorruptibility, and the mortal by immortality, that we might receive the adoption of sons?[87]

John Calvin puts this similarly in his *Institutes* while talking about the Lord's Supper:

> This is the wondrous exchange made by his boundless goodness. Having become with us the Son of Man, he has made us with himself sons of God. By his own descent to the earth he has prepared our ascent to heaven. Having received our mortality, he has bestowed on us his immortality. Having undertaken our weakness, he has made us strong in his strength. Having submitted to our poverty, he has transferred to us his riches. Having taken upon himself the burden of

86. Ibid., 548; V.XXI.1.
87. Ibid., 448–49;III.XIX.1.

> unrighteousness with which we were oppressed,
> he has clothed us with his righteousness.[88]

Finally, in the resurrection of Christ our corruption is overwhelmed by incorruption and our mortality with immortality:

> For the Lord, having been born "the First-begotten of the dead," and receiving into His bosom the ancient fathers, has regenerated them into the life of God, He having been made Himself the beginning of those that live, as Adam became the beginning of those who die.[89]

Irenaeus's emphasis on the resurrection of Christ is intentionally distinct from the gnostic denial of the body and Christ's resurrection. Bart Ehrman makes this clear when he writes, "Salvation does not come by worshiping the God of this world or accepting his creation. It comes by denying this world and rejecting the body that binds us to it."[90] Therefore, the

> entire point of salvation is to *escape* from this material world. A resurrection of a dead corpse brings the person back *into* the world of the creator. Since the point is to allow the soul to leave this world behind and enter into "the great and holy generation"—that is, the divine realm that transcends this world—a resurrection of the

---

88. Calvin, *Institutes*, 4.17.2.
89. Irenaeus, *Against Heresies*, 455; III.XXII.4.
90. Ehrman, *Christianity Turned*, 101.

body is the very last thing that Jesus, or any of his
true followers, would want.[91]

The restorative redemption brought by Christ applies
to the rest of creation as well. For the creation order will be
"restored to its primeval condition"[92] and not annihilated.[93]
In the words of N. T. Wright, "It is the resurrection . . . that
breaks open all other worldviews and demands that the
closed systems with which humans try to make sense of their
world must be held open to allow for the God who, having
created the world, has never for a moment abandoned it."[94]

This full-blown creational restorative redemption is
referred to by Hoekema in this way:

> If God would have to annihilate the present
> cosmos, Satan would have won a great victory,
> for then Satan would have succeeded in so dev-
> astatingly corrupting the present universe and
> the present earth that God could do nothing
> with it but blot it out of existence. But Satan was
> decisively defeated. God will reveal the full di-
> mensions of that defeat when he renews this very
> earth on which Satan deceived mankind, and fi-
> nally banishes from it all the results of Satan's evil
> work. God will maintain his creation. There will
> be continuity as well as discontinuity between
> the present earth and the new earth.[95]

91. Ibid., 110.

92. Irenaeus, *Against Heresies*, 561; V.XXXII.1.

93. Ibid., 566; V.XXXVI.1.

94. Wright, *Who Was Jesus*, 82.

95. Hoekema, "Heaven," http://www.ctlibrary.com/ct/2003/june
web-only/6-2-54.0.html.

Irenaeus goes further and describes this restorative redemption wrought by Christ Jesus: "He will renew the inheritance of the earth, and will re-organize the mystery of the glory of [His] sons."[96] Also, the earth will bear an abundance of produce:

> The predicted blessing, therefore, belongs unquestionably to the times of the kingdom, when the righteous shall bear rule upon their rising from the dead; when also the creation, having been renovated and set free, shall fructify with an abundance of all kinds of food, from the dew of heaven, and from the fertility of the earth.[97]

Even the animals will populate the earth, obeying and being in submission to their rightful masters, humankind.[98]

Here we see one of the major values of Irenaeus's Christology. Contrary to the gnostic push to disparage the physical and the created, Irenaeus's Christology affirms creation. As grace restores nature, humanity is brought back to God in Christ, body, soul, and spirit, and creation is renovated. That is because the "unity of God and man in the incarnate Christ hinges on the reality of the flesh of Christ, without which there could be no recapitulation of Adam."[99] By taking the initiative and drawing the creator and creature together in himself, Christ has turned away the alienation that came with the fall, thus bringing about "the union

---

96. Irenaeus, *Against Heresies*, 562; V.XXXIII.1.

97. Ibid., 562; V.XXXIII.3.

98. Ibid., 563; V.XXXIII.4.

99. Osborn, *Irenaeus*, 47.

and communion of God and man."[100] Even Calvin, whom Todd Billings says has very Irenaean tendencies, emphasizes that "participation in Christ's death is always followed by a participation in Christ's resurrection, which involves a fulfillment of the original telos of creation, the good 'substance' of human nature";[101] and "that redemption in Christ, the second Adam, fulfills and restores the creation; thus, in Christ human beings can be united to God."[102] Therefore, the way of restored relationship between God and human is not through "unmediated mystical knowledge,"[103] but through the restoring work of Christ's real incarnation and recapitulation.

In the final section of this chapter, we learn from Irenaeus the importance of Christians affirming and announcing these things:

1. The incarnation is the decisive moment when God begins healing humanity's fallen nature and the creation's bondage and brokenness;

2. The incarnation is the vital act of God in which he initiates the reconciliation of God and humankind;[104]

3. The incarnation, life, death, resurrection, and ascension of Christ redemptively recapitulate the Adamic predicament: Christ's obedience undoes Adam's disobedience;

100. Irenaeus, *Against Heresies*, 527; V.I.1.

101. Billings, "John Calvin," 203.

102. Billings, *Calvin, Participation*, 49.

103. Barnstone and Meyer, *Gnostic Bible*, 16.

104. It doesn't seem from my reading that Irenaeus asserted any kind of universalism. Therefore my conclusions should not be taken in a universalistic way.

4. The restorative redemption of Christ applies to creation: orthodox Christology is creation-affirming.

CONCLUSION

Though much more could be said about Irenaeus's way of dealing with the gnostics, this Christological approach seems, at present, to be the place to begin:

1. The place to meet God, behind whom there is no other God, is this flesh-and-blood man, Jesus Christ.

2. The Jesus of history and the Christ of faith are one and the same person, and to separate them is to fall into a gnostic trap.

3. We come to know this man, Jesus Christ, in the Scriptures, the Old Testament wrapped up in and read through the Apostolic tradition as recorded in the four Gospels and the rest of the New Testament writings.

4. Restoring and reclaiming the good creation is part and parcel of Christ's redemptive work. This is seen in the Word of God taking to himself the creation and humanity, and by his incarnation, recapitulating life, death, and resurrection, he inaugurates the undoing of Adam's fall and its creational consequences.

For the above-mentioned reasons, then, Osborne is correct when he affirms that from Irenaeus "a whole theology of physical redemption arises. . . . Futility and pessimism belong to those who deny the salvation of the flesh (5.2.2)."[105]

---

105. Osborn, *Irenaeus*, 228.

5

Conclusion

But to fail here, is not mere life or death. It is that we become as him; that we henceforward become foul things of the night like him—without heart or conscience, preying on the bodies and the souls of those we love best [Dr. Van Helsing, emphasizing the importance of finding Count Dracula and neutralizing him].[1]

W HEN I began this study, I had conflicted assumptions. On the one hand, it appeared to me that the congregation I pastor was thoroughly unmovable in regard to the Jesus of history who is the Christ of faith. I was also confident that they would be able to intelligently resist any challenges to Jesus' deity, or to the historical authenticity and authority of the canonical Gospels. Yet, on the other hand, as Dan Brown's book, *The Da Vinci Code*, became increasingly popular, I was sensing areas of doubt or confusion that might disable some folk's ability to "give a defense to everyone who asks [them] a reason for the hope that is in [them]."[2]

1. Stoker, *Dracula*, 281.
2. 1 Pet 3:15.

As this study unfolded, and I broadened my research into other churches, it became clear that many Christians do have a solid grip on the essential aspects of the Christian faith and on who Jesus Christ really is. But it also became obvious that there were spots that needed to be strengthened. The most outstanding subjects, across denominational and congregational lines, were (1) the singularly significant historical events in the life of the Lord Jesus Christ, (2) the uniqueness of the divinity of Jesus, (3) the authenticity of the canonical Gospels, (4) the pro-creation ramifications of Christ's redemptive vocation, and (5) how to respond successfully to Gnostic oppositions to both the uniqueness of "our great God and Savior Jesus Christ" and the genuinely authoritative place of the canonical Gospels.[3]

The first chapter addressed the danger of ancient and present Gnosticism, specifically how Gnosticism challenges the orthodox belief in Jesus as the *sui generis* Son of God described in the canonical Gospels. It was shown how this challenge was partly grounded on the Gnostic aversion to creation and history, and partly on a supposed internal pneumatic authority.

The second chapter surveyed three local congregations of diverse denominational backgrounds, to uncover possible patterns of deficiency in discernment as well as theology. The results of the survey showed that the churches generally fared well, but a significant portion of parishioners still lacked sufficient coaching for withstanding modern Gnostic trends.

The third chapter examined the New Testament letter of Jude to see what it contained that might be helpful in

3. Titus 2:13.

guiding a congregation to defend against the influences and challenges posed by alternative "Christianities" like neo-Gnosticism. The predominant medicine Jude prescribed was remembering and recalling the apostolic faith that has been passed on once for all to the believers and is found in the Christian Scriptures.

The fourth chapter explored Irenaeus's work *Against Heresies*, which specifically refuted Gnosticism's challenges. The primary focus was on the one issue where modern Gnosticism raises its stiffest challenge today, and how Irenaeus dealt with it: Christology.

This final chapter will address how a pastor and congregation can draw from this study to strengthen their ability and resolve in answering the problems posed by modern Gnosticism in the present day. My aim here is to extract from Jude's principle of remembering and reminding, as well Irenaeus's robust Christology, through the use of preaching, sacraments, catechesis, confession of faith, and finally, by building together on the most holy faith.[4]

PREACHING

The late-nineteenth-century Southern Presbyterian theologian, R. L. Dabney, asserted that "the state of the pulpit may always be taken as an index of that of the Church. Whenever the pulpit is evangelical, the piety of the people is in some degree healthy; a perversion of the pulpit is surely followed by spiritual apostasy in the Church."[5] Therefore,

4. Much of my thinking in this chapter was fortified by J. Todd Billings, in his book, *The Word of God for the People of God*.

5. Dabney, *Evangelical Eloquence*, 27.

to build up the strength and stamina of the congregation for resisting the assaults of modern Gnosticism, preaching has a primary role to play. To be faithful to our Lord and to the congregation,[6] preaching must be biblical, theological, apologetic, and evangelical, for, "Preaching is theology coming through a man who is on fire."[7] Just as important, preaching must always come around to the Jesus Christ of faith and history.

Similarly, because the Holy Scriptures are God-breathed, profitable for doctrine, reproof, correction, and instruction in righteousness, able to make one wise unto salvation,[8] and are also our "rule of faith and life,"[9] and where we meet the Jesus of history who is the Christ of faith, then the canonical Scriptures need to be the primary, singular source from which to preach. The preacher has "no biblical authority to say anything else" than what God says.[10] And because "hearts are transformed when people are confronted with the Word of God," then the preacher must be "committed to saying what God says."[11]

Therefore, keeping in mind the modern thrust of neo-Gnosticism, as well as carefully weighing our commission to preach, it is important to preach through the whole corpus of biblical books. That means spending as much "sermonic" time in the Old Testament as in the New.[12] In this way the

6. And for those who make solemn vows at their ordination, to be faithful to those vows.

7. Lloyd-Jones, *Preaching and Preachers*, 97.

8. 2 Tim 3: 15–16.

9. "Westminster Confession of Faith," I.2

10. Chapell, *Christ-Centered Preaching*, 23.

11. Ibid., 22.

12. My intentional pattern for preaching is to preach all the way

apostolic tradition, with the apostolic hermeneutic for reading the Hebrew Scriptures, can be demonstrated and rehearsed regularly. Steven Lawson agrees when he writes that "pastors must teach a comprehensive biblical message that is rooted in both the Old and New Testaments, focused on Christ, and full of doctrinal instruction."[13]

Likewise, it ought to be a chief aim to preach through one of the canonical Gospels regularly, maybe every second or third year. This way the people of the church can become better prepared to address modern Gnostic trends in their own thinking, as well as in others around them. It becomes especially valuable if the preaching stresses the historical authenticity of each particular Gospel and how that Gospel account says something specific about the Jesus Christ of faith and history. In addition, it will mean placing more emphasis on how the canonical Gospels follow the pattern of the passion of Christ as the interpretive structure, whereas a work such as *The Gospel of Thomas* does not.[14]

Yet solely hearing the Scriptures read and proclaimed, focusing on the auditory and cognitive, might simply lend itself to continuing Gnostic tendencies, especially with regard to the Gnostic notion that salvation is not salvation from sin but salvation from ignorance.[15] Therefore the faithful pastor and congregation must move beyond the simply analytical. Jesus himself gave two very earthly and physical rites to be enjoyed by his people: baptism with water and

through a New Testament book, and then preach through an Old Testament one. That keeps me and the congregation in the whole Bible.

13. Lawson, *Famine*, 38.

14. Behr, *Mystery*, 62–64.

15. Ehrman, *Christianity Turned*, 84.

the supper of bread and wine. And these two are inextricably bound up with the Holy Word declared: "Orthodoxy, however, in all its twists and turns, is pointed in one direction, that of Jesus Christ the incarnate Son of God. The one direction is guaranteed through the orthodox community's regular celebration of Word and Sacrament."[16]

SACRAMENTS

A reader may wonder how paying attention to and thoughtfully using the sacraments can be a useful remedy to correct Gnostic trends in a congregation. It seems to me that the increasing marginalization of the sacraments has happened simultaneously with the expansion of Gnostic trends in congregations. If Gnosticism is anticosmic dualism, sacraments are very earth-and-heaven-bound, physical rites. To thoughtfully, seriously expand the one will necessitate the diminishment of the other, and this goes both ways. R. R. Reno notes something similar when he writes:

> Few Christians are gnostics in the classical sense of the term. After all, the Old Testament is part of the Christian scripture, and the embodied, ritual life of the church claims to embody the spiritual power of salvation.[17] Nonetheless, modern Christianity has tended toward a functional gnosticism in which the divine plan is understood as a progressive universalizing and

16. Lee, *Protestant Gnostics*, 176.

17. Though I would disagree with Reno about the sacraments embodying the spiritual power of salvation, I agree with the "Westminster Confession of Faith" that the sacraments are God's ordinary and outward means of communicating to us the benefits of Christ's redemption.

spiritualizing of religion. Christianity may have rituals, but it is a religion of love rather than a preoccupation with bodily marks and signs. Fine sentiments and good intentions, so this line of thought reasons, supersede what are taken to be empty rituals.[18]

As Gnostic trends increase in a congregation (or denomination), there will be a marginalizing of the physical, sacred rites. Consequently, the thoughtful, serious administration of the sacraments will truly become a medicinal remedy. That is the approach behind what follows.

Following the influence of Augustine, the sacred rites given to the church by Jesus have been called "visible signs of invisible grace" by many. They represent, through things we can see, touch, feel, taste, smell (water, bread, wine), what God does in the hearts and lives of his people. In other words, what is promised by God in his Holy Scriptures accompanies the outward action and is made effective by the Holy Spirit working on and in those who believe. The "Westminster Shorter Catechism" addresses the sacraments this way:

> *How do the sacraments become effectual means of salvation?* The sacraments become effectual means of salvation, not from any virtue in them, or in him that doth administer them; but only by the blessing of Christ, and the working of his Spirit in them that by faith receive them. *What is a sacrament?* A sacrament is an holy ordinance instituted by Christ, wherein, by sensible signs,

18. Reno, *Genesis*, 176.

> Christ, and the benefits of the new covenant, are
> represented, sealed, and applied to believers.[19]

In other words, the Holy Scriptures along with the sacraments "are the tangible, audible, and edible Word of God. They are the tangible, audible, and edible promises of God."[20]

A minister in the Presbyterian Church in America (PCA) is bound to observe only two sacraments. His second ordination vow affirms that he holds to the Confession of Faith and Catechisms of the PCA as the system of doctrine taught in the Scriptures.[21] And the Confession acknowledges only the dominical rites of baptism and the Lord's Supper as sacraments. Therefore, I will limit myself to these two rites.

The initiatory rite is baptism with water. In Reformed churches, baptism is a public event "which concerns the whole congregation to which the person baptized is admitted."[22] Though it has often been administered at the beginning of a service in many traditions, yet to show how the word and sacrament go together, it would be quite fitting to baptize after the sermon but before the Eucharist.[23] By having the person to be baptized come forward and stand by the Lord's table to receive baptism would visibly show that the one being baptized is coming in response to the word proclaimed. Once the person has been drenched with

19. 91 and 92. See also *The Book of Common Prayer*, "Articles of Religion," Article XXV.

20. Wilken, "Promise-Driven Church," 23.

21. *Book of Church Order*, chapter 21, paragraph 5.2

22. Bromiley, *Sacramental Teaching*, 38.

23. In some churches, baptism occurs at the entrance to the nave; in others, up close to the pulpit and the table.

plenty of water in the name of the Father, and of the Son, and of the Holy Spirit,[24] it would be salutary for the minister to place his hand on the baptizand's shoulder or head and charge her with Galatians 3:26–27, 2:20 and Romans 6:11. For example:

> Remember, you have become a child of God by faith in Christ Jesus, you are now clothed with Jesus Christ in your baptism. Therefore, you have been crucified with Christ, it is no longer you who lives, but Christ lives in you. And the life which you now live in the flesh, live by faith in the Son of God who loved you and gave himself for you. Reckon yourself to be dead, indeed, unto sin, but alive to God in Christ Jesus our Lord. Amen.

By doing this, the minister is vocally and publicly declaring the identification of the baptized person with the Christ of faith and history. This will visibly and audibly strengthen the truth that "baptism is here a summons to be what we are, to enter more and more into the fullness of identification with Christ in his death and resurrection," both for the one being baptized and those hearing and seeing it.[25]

Also, in this act of baptism it is essential to stress that the baptizand, as well as all those who are observing and have already been baptized, are born into the new, visible, concrete community of Christ's covenant people. To remind everyone that Christian baptism, ritually and of-

24. A pitcher of water might be poured over them, just as disciples were baptized with the Holy Spirit who was poured out on them at Pentecost (Acts 2:17–18, 33).

25. Bromiley, *Children of Promise*, 85.

ficially, places them in continuity with the people of God under the old covenant, as well as with his people in the new throughout the last two thousand years. This rather objective "new birth" is what Philip Lee refers to when he writes: "The person is born again not in a sense of a psycho-emotional experience, but in the sense that from the moment of baptism his or her entire orientation and destiny has to do with the holy community led by Christ."[26] In the communal event of baptism, the pastor, the person being baptized, and the congregation are corporately renouncing the Gnostic notion that the church is an "organization of and for the individual."[27]

Because of the ongoing importance of the sacraments in the life of the church, coming to enjoy the Lord's Supper weekly will be advantageous. Not only does this fit in with Jesus' descriptive "as often as you do this,"[28] but it also ties in nicely with the early pattern of disciples who "continued steadfastly in the . . . breaking of bread."[29] Finally, if observed every Lord's Day, the Eucharist becomes the enacted conclusion of the whole worship assembly, where the congregation is invited to receive the Lord Jesus by faith.

The PCA minister is charged with declaring who may and who may not commune as the congregation prepares to partake. [30] The declarative act of fencing of the table weekly

26. Lee, *Protestant Gnostics*, 253.

27. Ibid., 158.

28. 1 Cor 11:25.

29. Acts 2:42.

30. This is often designated as "fencing the table," and it has a long history. In the earlier church liturgies the catechumens were dismissed before the Eucharist. Also, St. Ambrose withheld the

places before the congregation the fact that the Lord's Supper is not an automatic right. Instead, it requires living communion in the family of God with the family of God, as well as a desire for increasing sanctification, all of which is very antidocetic and antignostic. The minister who fences the table should remind the gathered of the historical sacrifice of Christ in his incarnation, holy life and crucifixion, as well as the historical triumph of Christ in his resurrection. Fencing the table is not only about saying who is excluded, but also an invitation to the congregation to eat and drink the mercy of God, who comes to us as we eat the bread and drink wine in faith with thanksgiving. To emphasize this last thought, after the prayer of consecration is offered, the minister might charge the congregation, in words modified from the 1979 *Book of Common Prayer*: "The gifts of God, for the people of God, that you and I may grow in the grace of God. Take them in remembrance that Christ died for you, and feed on him in your hearts by faith, with thanksgiving."[31]

As baptism "is the sacrament of initiation" into the communion of the family of God, the supper "is the sacrament of continuing communion in the family of God."[32] This corporate aspect of the Eucharist is one place where many congregations likely need to build. Reformed inclinations are to individualize and dehistoricize the Eucharist, turning it into a personal, pietistic devotional time. One way to overcome this and recommunalize the Eucharist is

Eucharist from the Emperor who had commissioned the slaughter of the Thessalonikans.

31. 338.

32. Clowney, *Church*, 286.

to initiate congregational singing during the distribution of the bread and the wine. Singing of a hymn about Christ and his love for us lends itself to thinking more broadly than about our own personal selves. We are drawn out of our secluded inner worlds by the voices around us singing the same hymn, holding the bread in their hands, or the cup of wine, waiting to partake.

Participating in the Lord's Supper weekly and observing the physical and visible actions of baptism help to drive home the tangible, audible, and edible promises of God in Jesus Christ. Also, in order to capitalize on the highly anti-docetic nature of our faith, it would be good to remind the congregation that Jesus Christ, having assumed our whole humanity, is saving us body and soul. [33] Grace is restoring and transforming nature.[34] Finally, through these sacraments, the minds and thoughts of the people should be repeatedly drawn to the corporate nature of our faith. This is not just an immediate incorporation but a truly catholic incorporation, since we share these sacraments with Christ's people throughout the ages, even with those of the Old Testament, as St. Paul stresses:

> Moreover, brethren, I do not want you to be unaware that all our fathers were under the cloud, all passed through the sea, all were baptized into Moses in the cloud and in the sea, all ate the same spiritual food, and all drank the same spiritual drink. For they drank of that spiritual Rock that followed them, and that Rock was Christ.[35]

33. Boersma, *Violence*, 122.

34. Billings, *Calvin, Participation*, 45–49.

35. 1 Cor 10:1–4.

But rites must be accompanied with words, or they quickly fall into magical, vacuous rituals. Therefore, with the Word of God proclaimed, and the Word of God presented to our senses in the sacraments, the congregation ought to vocalize and rehearse the pattern of sound words once for all delivered to the people of God.[36]

CONFESSION OF FAITH

The ancient confessions of faith, like the Nicene Creed and the Apostles' Creed, emphasize creation, monotheism, the historical passion, resurrection, ascension, and return of Christ, as well as the place of the church in God's economy. All of these accentuate an antignostic profession of belief. Therefore, as a congregation gathers weekly for worship, a confession of faith should be repeated in every worship assembly after the sermon and before the sacraments.[37] Since beginning this study on modern Gnosticism, I have made it a point to do the same confession all month long, and then to change to another one each month, for the sake of retention and freshness. We use the two major creeds, the Nicene and the Apostles'. In addition, we also use four other confessions. Each of these creedal statements revolves around what God has done for us in Jesus Christ historically. For example, my congregation's favorite is from an early Reformation catechism:

36. Even though I am only now mentioning confessing our faith, the order in worship should be: (1) word proclaimed; (2) faith confessed; (3) sacraments received.

37. Thompson, *Liturgies*, 191.

> What is your only comfort in life and in death?
> That I, with body and soul, both in life and in
> death, am not my own, but belong to my faithful
> Savior Jesus Christ, who with His precious blood
> has fully satisfied for all my sins, and redeemed me
> from all the power of the devil; and so preserves
> me that without the will of my Father in heaven
> not a hair can fall from my head; indeed, that
> all things must work together for my salvation.
> Wherefore, by His Holy Spirit, He also assures me
> of eternal life, and makes me heartily willing and
> ready from now on to live unto Him.[38]

The other three creedal statements I have crafted for
our congregation are renditions of Scripture: Galatians 2:20;
Philippians 2:5–11; and Colossians 1:15–23a.[39] As observed
in chapter three, remembering the apostles' passed-on
tradition is an important aspect for fending off the entice-
ments of those who are seeking to draw us away from the
faith once for all delivered to the saints. Using sound and
solid creedal statements weekly and corporately is a lively
way that a congregation can remember, recall, and remind
one another faithfully.

The point of these previous three sections has been
to accentuate worship that should be antidocetic and antignostic, on the negative side; as well as confessional, corporate, and theological on the positive. The ancient maxim,
lex orandi, lex credendi est is behind this thought.[40] As Hart
points out, "Worship always reflects a people's conception

---

38. *Heidelberg Catechism*, Q and A 1.

39. These creedal statements can be found in Appendix B.

40. Translated, this means: "the language of prayer is the language
of faith."

of God. . . . Worship is not a matter of taste; it is a statement of theological conviction about who God is and who we are as his covenant people."[41]

Along with the corporate, weekly worship of the congregation, there are other ways to help a church become stronger in withstanding the modern Gnostic trends of our day. The most obvious way to do this is by making sure that specific pro-creational, Christological orthodoxy finds its way into the central part of the public teaching of the church.

CATECHESIS

Another area that will help in reminding and recalling the apostolic faith for a congregation is catechesis. This is the process where the "Church teaches details about God," a knowledge "rooted in a lived faith that acts on what it knows."[42] It is a formation process for "both the new in faith and the more mature."[43] Wholesome catechesis should be approached at three levels concurrently: evangelism, catechetical teaching, and catechetical preaching.

Evangelism

Because evangelism is one of the first places Christians get to tell others about the Christian faith, it is an excellent spot to put forth the basics. Christians need to be taught what the content of the Gospel is before they go out and tell others. And when they do declare the Gospel in an intentionally patterned way, it forms the foundation in both the teller

41. Hart, *Recovering Mother Kirk*, 79.
42. Dawn, *Royal Waste of Time*, 245.
43. Ibid., 251.

and receiver, upon which everything else hangs. Catechesis begins here. One of the best evangelism approaches I have seen to date is *The Two Ways to Live: The Choice We all Face* by Matthias Media out of Australia.

This material lays out the Gospel in a simple format that includes the content of much of the larger biblical story:

> The message at the heart of Christianity is really quite simple—simple enough to be outlined in a few pages. It is a message from the Bible about God and his son, Jesus. It is about life and death, and the choice that we all face. And it all begins with a loving creator God.[44]

Two Ways to Live then follows a logical summary:

1. God is the creator; humanity rules under his authority.

2. Humanity rebels, wishing to run things its own way.

3. God judges (and will judge) humanity for this rebellion.

4. In his love, God sends Jesus to die as an atoning sacrifice.

5. In his power, God raises Jesus to life as ruler and judge.

6. This presents us with a challenge to repent and believe.[45]

Even though the *Two Ways to Live* material is not as full as it could be, nevertheless, it begins in a fashion that

44. Jensen and Payne, *Choices We All Face*, 1.
45. Jensen and Payne, *Know and Share*, 9.

undermines Gnosticism's anticosmic dualism. [46] The good God made a good creation. Sin is not programmed into the creation but comes later, as a result of man's rebellion. The way out is not to escape from creation, but to experience liberation through the death and resurrection of Jesus Christ. All very solidly biblical, antignostic points!

By approaching evangelism in the manner Matthias Media does, the Christian is able to show a whole different way of seeing the world. The person hearing the Gospel in this way hears a different story, a different "plausibility structure," than the one modern evolutionary determinism or New Age mysticism touts. [47] If they come to be converted, then this is part of their initial introduction to the Christian faith.

Also, the Christian who is taught all of this material benefits immensely. She begins seeing that each piece is an important part of the true story of what God is doing to remedy creation's and humanity's condition. By the Christian memorizing this simple summary, she is then being trained to hear the Bible through this structural grid (good creation, fall, redemption). Therefore, evangelism and evangelism training is a first stage of catechesis.

46. There's no mention of the goal of Christ's redemptive work beyond just for the individual; no church, sacraments, nor the place of creation in Christ's work. Yet there is plenty of room to add all of these things, both in the evangelism training and the presentation to non-Christians.

47. Newbigin, *Gospel*, 53.

Catechetical Instruction

A second level of catechesis is catechetical instruction. Several Protestant traditions have a custom of using catechisms. [48] A catechism is theology in a question-and-answer format. If questions and answers are not too wordy, they can be retained by children, teens, and adults with a minimal amount of effort. Originally, catechisms were meant to be used at home by parents with their children, which is very fitting and essential. Nevertheless, portions of a particular tradition's catechism can be added to the formal worship assembly for all the participants to become familiar with the pattern of the teaching. There are also Sunday School curricula that teach just the catechism for children and teens.[49]

Whether a specific tradition has a catechism or not, there are other ways to teach the Christian faith in a systematic manner. For example, the leadership of a congregation could plan out a cyclical order of topics for teen and adult Christian education. In our congregation I have put in motion a plan where every two to three years we spend at least a four-month period dealing with apologetics in one form or another. Somewhere in the cycle, maybe every second or third round, it would be important to put into the apologetic portion what we mean by the Holy Scriptures of the Old and New Testaments being the infallible and inerrant Word of God. In this instructional category the leadership would want to address how we came by the Scriptures. It will then afford an occasion to explain how the church

48. Anglican, Lutheran, and Presbyterian, to name a few.

49. One example is the material put out by Great Commission Publications, 3640 Windsor Park Dr., Suwanee, GA.

came to recognize the canon of Scripture in the first centuries, how early the New Testament was compiled, and why the gnostic texts never made it in. Doing so will give an opening to show the distinctive texture of the Gospels (in contrast to gnostic "Gospels"). The leadership will be able to point out how the canonical Gospel accounts follow the apostolic pattern of drawing on the Hebrew Scriptures as a thesaurus, and a "compendium of the words and images with which" to "articulate the mystery of Christ, the Christ proclaimed 'in accordance with the scriptures.'"[50]

There are a number of other essential topics that the congregation's leadership would find important to repeat in a programmed way every two or three years. These topics can be addressed from various angles so that boredom doesn't set in, but they end up covering much of the same material. The leadership must shy away from the fear of repetition and actively rehearse the central aspects of the Christian faith. In doing so, the congregants will become increasingly more capable of recalling why we believe what we believe, and their ability to discern between good and evil will become genuinely solid, and personalized. [51]

Catechetical Preaching

One final level of catechesis is catechetical preaching. Some Reformed traditions do this by preaching through their catechism every year on Sunday evenings. That is one very intentional format to ensure that the congregation hears about many topics that are not normally covered in the

50. Behr, *Mystery*, 55.
51. Hebrews 5:14.

average Sunday morning preaching. Another design is to bring the catechism into the Sunday morning preaching where it fits the Scripture selection for the day. Though this design is more hit-and-miss than systematic, it exhibits for the congregation how the catechism flows out of biblical theology and is not imposed on the Scripture (a very important Protestant emphasis).

Regularly reiterating the basic, historical Christian faith is important. If the leadership hits a slump in this regard, it would be good to restudy the tenets of Gnosticism, what Gnostic trends look like in a local church, and how Jude and Irenaeus responded to the Gnostic challenges. In so doing, the leaders will be reminded of the importance of repetitiously affirming the basic, historical faith of Jesus Christ and exhibiting how the orthodox faith stands up against its challengers.

BUILDING TOGETHER
ON THE MOST HOLY FAITH

Lesslie Newbigin, in his book *The Gospel in a Pluralist Society*, has made an impressive case for the congregation as a major, living hermeneutic for the Gospel. [52] He points out,

> Jesus, as I said earlier, did not write a book but formed a community. This community has at its heart the remembering and rehearsing of his words and deeds, and the sacraments given by him through which it is enabled both to engraft new members into its life and to renew this life

---

52. Lesslie Newbigin was a missionary to India. His experience with Hindu culture makes his insights helpful in dealing with Gnosticism.

again and again through sharing in his risen
life through the body broken and the lifeblood
poured out. It exists in him and for him, He is
the center of its life. Its character is given to it,
when it is true to its nature, not by the characters
of its members but by his character. Insomuch as
it is true to its calling, it becomes the place where
men and women and children find that the gospel gives them the framework of understanding,
the "lenses" through which they are able to understand and cope with the world.[53]

Then Newbigin traces out six characteristics of a
church being true to its calling: (1) It will be a community
of praise, where the members are given over to liberating
reverence and are not focused on their own rights. (2) It will
be a community of truth, "not aligned to the techniques of
modern propaganda," but "the modesty, the sobriety, and the
realism which are proper to a disciple of Jesus." (3) It will be
a community that does not live for itself but immerses itself
in the concerns of its neighborhood: "It will be the church
for the specific place where it lives." (4) The congregation
being true to its calling will be a community where men
and women "are prepared for and sustained in the exercise
of the priesthood in the world." On Sunday it renews its
participation in Christ's priesthood, and then goes forth to
exercise this priesthood in the "daily business of the world."
(5) It will be a community of mutual responsibility. If the
church is going to advocate a new social order in a nation,
"it must itself be a new social order." (6) It will be a community of hope. The church lives in a world that is strug-

53. Newbigin, *Gospel*, 227.

gling with a famine of hope and widespread pessimism. By indwelling the gospel story, and being the community that is shaped by the gospel story, we flesh out a real "plausibility structure" that challenges the cultural atmosphere of pessimism, and we become ourselves enabled to steadily and confidently live in an "attitude of eager hope."[54]

Remember that Gnosticism, and its modern descendent, has imbibed in the story of alienation, of "the anguished discovery of man's cosmic solitude" in which God is not merely "extra-mundane and supra-mundane, but in his ultimate meaning contra-mundane."[55] Recall that in the Gnostic scheme, a person who possesses the gnosis is alienated from creation and fellow humans, because "the *pneumaticos*, 'spiritual' man, who does not belong to any objective scheme, is above the law, beyond good and evil, and a law unto himself in the power of his 'knowledge.'"[56] Therefore, the church that is attempting to be loyal to its calling will not be a church "of and for the individual."[57] Instead, it will be driven to be a communion in which alienation between human and God, and human and human, are overcome in Christ who "is our peace."[58]

This new community, drawn together around Jesus, knit together by the Holy Spirit, goes forth together to draw others into the household of the Father. Edmund Clowney is helpful in describing this God-created, Jesus-shaped, Spirit-knit togetherness that is a new humanity: "Every

54. Ibid., 227–32.

55. Jonas, *Gnostic Religion*, 251.

56. Ibid., 334.

57. Lee, *Protestant Gnostics*, 158.

58. Eph 2:14.

true church of Christ is a manifestation of the new people of God, composed of citizens of heaven, not of devout people forming their elite club."[59] That means that a given congregation that wants to be faithful to her Lord must see herself, not as a Rotary Club with a cross, but as the new-heavens-and-new-earth people, who are given to Jesus that he may send us into the world. And in sending us back into the world, we find we are participating in his giving himself "for the life of the world."[60]

But being this new-heavens-and-new-earth people means also that there is a new way in which we respond to one another, a new way that will be attractive to both the strangers and aliens in our world:

> Increasingly the ordered fellowship of the church becomes the sign of grace for the warring factions of a disordered world. Only as the church binds together those whom selfishness and hate have cut apart will its message be heard and its ministry of hope to the friendless be received.[61]

This, it seems to me, is where a church begins to actively take the modern Gnostic trends and turn them upside down and inside out. The wonderful exchange Christ Jesus made with us sets the agenda for us as his church. This exchange is beautifully described by John Calvin in the sixteenth century and an anonymous Christian in the second or third century:

59. Clowney, *Church*, 98.
60. John 6:51.
61. Clowney, *Church*, 16.

Submitting to our poverty, he has transferred to us his riches; assuming our weakness, he has strengthened us by his power; accepting our mortality, he has conferred on us his immortality; taking on himself the load of iniquity with which we were oppressed, he has clothed us with his righteousness; descending to the earth, he has prepared a way for our ascending to heaven; becoming with us the Son of Man, he has made us, with himself, the sons of God.[62]

But he was patient, he bore with us, and out of pity for us he took our sins upon himself. He gave up his own Son as a ransom for us, the holy one for the lawless, the innocent one for the wicked, the righteous one for the unrighteous, the imperishable one for the perishable, the immortal one for the mortal. 3. For what else could hide our sins but the righteousness of that one? 4. How could we who were lawless and impious be made upright except by the Son of God alone? 5. Oh, the sweet exchange! Oh, the inexpressible creation! Oh, the unexpected acts of beneficence! That the lawless deeds of many should be hidden by the one who was upright, and the righteousness of one should make upright the many who were lawless![63]

As the eternal Word and Son of God became human to strip away our alienation and bring about reconciliation with God, so the congregants are to strip the horizontal alienation of its power (whether economic, ethnic, educational, political, or social), and embrace one another. We

62. Calvin, *Institutes*, 643; IV.XVII.2.
63. "Epistle to Diognetus," 151.

are to chip in to help each other in times of difficulty. We must aim to draw in others of diverse ethnic backgrounds. As we together are dressed in Christ at baptism,[64] so we ought to worship and serve together, not holding the faith of our Lord Jesus with partiality.[65] Those who are better off financially should find their joy in giving generously to the Mercy Ministry Fund, or to help the baptized young single mother with three children meet her bills, so she can finish school and get her business certificate. Thus they will be rich in good works.[66] The older couple whose own children have spurned the faith and rejected marriage and child-birth are to turn their grandparenting desires into means of redemptive loving of other children who have no father or no mother, or whose daddy is off to the war in Iraq or Afghanistan. In other words, this is to be a church "for the specific place where it lives."[67]

Because belief and behavior live and die with one an-other, it is important that the congregation must seek to live out its faith in the God who made a good creation and has taken on that creation, to redeem it by becoming man. In this way he has begun our reconciliation and is overturning our alienation, especially in drawing that alienation into his real space-and-time cross:

> and by Him to reconcile all things to Himself, by Him, whether things on earth or things in heaven, having made peace through the blood of His cross. And you, who once were alienated

64. Gal 3:26–27.
65. Jas 2:1.
66. 1 Tim 6:18.
67. Newbigin, *Gospel*, 229.

> and enemies in your mind by wicked works, yet
> now He has reconciled in the body of His flesh
> through death, to present you holy, and blame-
> less, and above reproach in His sight.[68]

Therefore, "The true drawing power of the church transcends the cultural enclaves of contemporary society to dissolve the hatreds of a fallen world in the love of Christ."[69] This is where we must live out our faith, dissolving the hatreds of this fallen world in the love of Christ.

CONCLUSION

It should go without saying, but none of the items mentioned in this chapter work automatically, whether done separately or as a whole. Every aspect needs the blessing of Christ and the working of his Spirit. Every facet must be drenched with prayer. But we must intentionally and confidently apply ourselves, as leaders, to these functions. That is apostolic ministry! To "give ourselves continually to prayer and to the ministry of the word."[70]

In this chapter, I have given some examples of how the leadership and the congregation can begin actively responding to the dangerous trends of neo-Gnosticism, specifically with regard to preaching, the use of the sacraments, confessions of faith, and catechesis; and finally what it means for a congregation to be building upon our most holy faith by striving to be a church loyal to its calling.

---

68. Col 1:20–22.
69. Clowney, *Church*, 164.
70. Acts 6:4.

Appendix A

Survey

Below shows the survey I used with the three congregations and how they answered. The makeup of the congregations is expressed in chapter 2, as well as the overall analysis. This will simply be the mechanical aspects of the survey, several of the responses, the rationale behind the questions, and how I read the responses.

During one of the surveys, there was a group of four people who would not identify any denominational or congregational affiliation. They will be identified in the results below as "Other."

These survey questions were based on the primary ideas of Gnosticism as spelled out in chapter 1. I admit to not being any kind of professional statistician. These were questions that seemed to be worth asking, and the answers were worth reading. There may very well be other ways to interpret this material, but within the context of things I have been hearing and reading among local Christians (see the Introduction to this book), I think these results get very close to the truth of what is going on within local congregations.

SURVEY

Questions 1 and 2

The first two questions dealt with *The Da Vinci Code*. My intention behind them was to estimate the impact of the challenges to the Christian faith made by that book. I was trying to get a sense of how many people knew someone who had read the book, and if these acquaintances had brought forward any of the challenges from the book.

Question 1 asked, "Have you met anyone who has talked about the book *The Da Vinci Code*?"

In two of the churches and among the "other" group, over 70 percent knew someone who had read the book. Only 40 percent of Church C respondents had met anyone who had read it.

Question 2 asked, "What was their perception of the book? (If you have met more than one, describe as best you can, the various perceptions. Only use about two or three sentences)."

The participants who answered this question wrote replies that ranged from very negative to very positive. Most of their friends or acquaintances praised it for its readability, said that it was "a page-turning mystery," that it was "excellent writing—couldn't put it down." Yet several said that their friends noted it had "a lot of discrepancies," or that they "took it as a knock against Christianity." A few of the answerers said their friends either "thought it was false," or "that there may be some truth in it." Some respondents noted that the book caused their friends "confusion" and raised lots of "questions."

Question 3

"If your son came home from college this weekend and made these following statements, how might you answer him?

    A. The Christian teaching that *Jesus is one being with God* was forced onto Christianity only by a vote at the Council of Nicea in 325 A.D.

    B. The biblical Gospels are really mythical retellings of Jesus by some Christians who wrote so long after the described events that they couldn't really know what happened.

    C. The *Gospel According to Thomas* is just as valid in understanding Jesus as the biblical Gospels."

QUESTION 3A

The answers to the first scenario were decidedly weighted toward a Bible or faith answer of some kind. One person commented, "Faith not reason, Son. All Scripture is God-breathed, it states He is one." Several made similar faith-statements like, "Not so. The Bible says so." The historically-based replies were very simple, but they seemed to display a sense that some people knew something about the Council of Nicea and how the canon of Scripture came about. One respondent simply challenged the challenge with, "Where did you get your information?"

QUESTION 3B

The answers for the second part of the question showed more willingness to wrestle with the challenge on historical grounds. One person said that there was "more proof for the historicity of the Gospels than for the historicity of Julius Caesar's life and career." Another person responded, "The authenticity of historical documents is validated by the # (*sic*) of like testimonies and the time span between the event & the record—there are 100's more for the Gospel of Christ than most historical documents." Several people made faith-statements along the lines either that the Bible is the inspired Word of God and/or they would take this imaginary son to the Word of God. Finally, a few made other comments, such as it was "a lie from Satan." But there were other comments that were thoughtful in other directions. For example, one replied, "Who's (*sic*) assessment is that? And what qualifies their statement?"

QUESTION 3C

The third part of the question also evoked varied responses, with the largest portions falling into the category of canonization. Some made no response at all. With regard to the category of canonization, one stated, "It is a gnostic gospel written several hundred years after the Biblical Gospels and stemmed from a perverted teachings (*sic*) of a gnostic sect." Another responded that comparing the message of *The Gospel of Thomas* with the canonical Gospels would settle the issue. After the survey was completed, during a rather informal discussion with some of the respondents, it came out that many had not read the *Gospel of Thomas*.

Question 4

"True spiritual insight is built on and shaped by the truth which the apostles of Jesus taught, no matter what I have experienced.

    A. If this is true, please explain why in one or two sentences.

    B. If this is untrue, please explain why in one or two sentences."

With the question worded in this way the answers fell heavily, though not unanimously, in the realm of some sense of what truth is, no matter what one may experience. Someone wrote that true spiritual insight is "built on, and shaped by the truth which the apostles of Jesus taught" and not experience. Others stated: "The Gospel was and is inspired by God, and is the truth whether you reach an emotional high or not." "Our faith is built on historical facts not feelings or experiences." "The teaching of the apostles <u>is</u> the truth. Not a springboard for inventing our own spirituality. It is the ground and pillar of the truth."

A few people turned this either/or question into a both/and. For example, one wrote, "Truth is truth, whether you believe it or not. That is what makes it truth. But it is a safe assumption that God uses the truth of His Word and the experiences in our lives to allow us to know Him more." But then there were those who specifically stated "feeling" and "experiences" as the key for "true spiritual insight." One even made the apostles the receivers of experiences, and their experiences become the standard. This is simply staying within the subjective realm while placing the subjective experience criteria on the shoulders of others perceived as more valid. One person answered in such a way that I had no idea how to interpret what the answer meant, so it was placed in the "Uncertain" category.

Question 5

"Which of the following statements do you feel are most true to you? (Circle as many as apply):

A. Because we are in God's image, we have a divine spark in us.

B. We have direct access to God and don't need anything or anyone to make the way open to God for us.

C. We can actually get to know God on His terms.

D. I feel that God speaks to me personally, and directs me in fresh ways.

E. The body is the prison house of the soul.

F. More important than the historical Jesus is an encounter with the living Christ.

G. Having an inner vision of the Lord is just as important as the words of the New Testament.

Would you please explain your answer(s) here? Thank you."

The comments from Church A help to define some of their answers. Two of the comments for the "D" answers modified their votes so that they could actually fit with "C." For example, one simply added the words, "through Scripture" to the question, and the other wrote next to the

question, "Thru (*sic*) His Word." These same two respondents did not circle "C," but their written comments could
be added to the overall affirmation of "C." One person commented about "E" with this statement, "The body is only a
temporary shell for a soul that will live forever." And the
other "E" person made this note, "In some way." One response turned "F" around by stating, "Many people in history saw Jesus (physically), but unless God called them to
repentance they were not saved. While Christ is an important historical figure, He is also Savior of the world." Finally,
one person did not circle any of the letters, but wrote this
comment, "None are true."

The responses of Church B present a different emphasis. When permitted to explain their answers, five re-
frained from any written statements. One person caught
where many of these questions came from and stated, "It all
sounds 'New Age' & not Scriptural." Another put this statement next to letter A: "No. Gnostic belief." And then that
same person answered "B" in the affirmative and added,
"Jesus made the way." One only circled "C" and then offered
this statement, "What we know of God has been revealed
to us by His actions in history, particularly the history of
Israel & in His incarnation in Jesus the Christ." And one
who circled both "C" and "D" wrote, "I can only get to God
on his terms. His term is through Jesus Christ." Another
person who affirmed "C," "D," "E," and "F" added this comment: "though He was not giving us divinity He will stoop
to our level." Three other respondents simply mentioned
some subjective aspect of their answer, like; "I pray and ask
God for guidance." Some from Church B comprehended
the New Age and gnostic leanings in these statements, and

there were others who were pronounced in their confidence that personal experience was not the primary directive part of the Christian faith. Still, there were many responses that leaned heavily toward their belief that their experience of "the living Christ" was far more important than the historical Jesus and his actions.

Church C's written comments coupled with their circled answers exhibit tension or balance. For example, one person who had marked "B," "C," "D," and "F," explained by writing, "Jesus has interceded for us. We have direct access to God thru prayer & reading his Word. We have to obey His commandments & He will guide & direct us." Another person who actually responded in the affirmative for "A-G" qualified "B" by writing, "B-Scripture is of no private interpretation . . ." And another person qualified their answer by writing, "Jesus died for us to be able to be in God's presence." Two other respondents, though, only reaffirmed the subjective aspect of their answers in their written responses.

Of those whom I have categorized as "Other," there were only two who wrote comments. One wrote, in commenting on the two letters they circled: "A: People fired up for God stand out amongst others." I was unsure how to take this answer, but it might be that the use of "divine spark" in the question was asked poorly or simply misunderstood. "D: I am personal with God b/c know (*sic*) one knows my heart like he does." The other person who wrote an explanation stressed that the Spirit of God resides "in one's body—it is by the Spirit of God that I am led."

Question 6

"Which of the following statements do you feel is more important for you?

 A. Jesus Christ, the Son of God, died on a cross outside of Jerusalem about 2,000 years ago.

 B. I have a real and living relationship with God.

It would be really helpful if you would quickly explain your answer here."

Church A and those in the Other category weighed in heavily (approximately 70 percent) on the side of basing personal experience on the historical actions of God in Jesus Christ. In other words, they circled both "A" and "B." Several of those responding stated something along these lines: "Unless A) above is true, I could have no living relationship w/ God." Those from Church A who circled only "B" made written statements that played up the experience of "B" over the actions of God in Jesus Christ. For example, one wrote, "Having a personal relationship with Christ (the Resurrected Savior) is most important of all." In several instances, the responses pulled together "A" and "B," making the personal relationship with God dependent on the historical action of Jesus' crucifixion.

Church B and Church C answered in very pronounced ways. The greater amount either circled "A" (20 to 30 percent) or "B" (50 to 60 percent). Only a small number marked both "A" and "B." This, it seems to me, is very significant. Many of those who thought "A" was more important made similar comments to those mentioned above. One person commented, "If Jesus Christ did not die on a cross outside of Jerusalem 2000 years (*sic*) I cannot have a relationship with Him. Everything depends on the Cross." But of those who marked "B" alone, there was a strong current of emphasis on experience either being primary over the historical event of Jesus, or the historical has relatively no value. For example, some wrote statements like this: "B. Knowing & Loving Christ (God) is necessary for real spiritual salvation. A. Is a historical fact." Another wrote, "The fact Jesus died is not as important as statement B."

CONCLUSION

Once the survey was conducted, I taught a class on Gnosticism. All the survey respondents attended those classes and began to express a growing comprehension of what the survey was asking. The informal discussions that arose were very encouraging and insightful.

Appendix B

Alternative Confessions of Faith

A s NOTED in the fifth chapter, there are other confessions of faith Providence Presbyterian Church uses
regularly. Besides the Apostles' and the Nicene Creed,
there is the first question and answer to the Heidelberg
Catechism. And the following are other confessions used
regularly. These are Bible confessions intended to reinforce
the apostolic tradition and rule of faith.

1. Minister: Dear Children of God, declare what you
   believe!

ALL: I have been crucified with Christ; it is no longer
I who live, but Christ lives in me; and the life which I now
live in the flesh I live by faith in the Son of God, who loved
me and gave Himself for me (Galatians 2:20).

2. Minister: Dear Children of God, confess now your
   common faith.

ALL: I believe that Jesus Christ, being in the form
of God, did not consider it robbery to be equal with God,
but made Himself of no reputation, taking the form of a
bondservant, and coming in the likeness of men. And being
found in appearance as a man, He humbled Himself and

became obedient to the point of death, even the death of the cross. Therefore God also has highly exalted Him and given Him the name which is above every name, that at the name of Jesus every knee should bow, of those in heaven, and of those on earth, and of those under the earth, and that every tongue should confess that Jesus Christ is Lord, to the glory of God the Father. Amen (Philippians 2:6–11).

3. Minister: Let us now profess our common faith in response to God's Word:

ALL: I believe that Jesus Christ is the image of the invisible God, the firstborn over all creation. For by Him all things were created that are in heaven and that are on earth, visible and invisible, whether thrones or dominions or principalities or powers. All things were created through Him and for Him. And He is before all things, and in Him all things consist. And He is the head of the body, the church, who is the beginning, the firstborn from the dead, that in all things He may have the preeminence.

I believe that it pleased the Father that in Jesus all the fullness should dwell, and by Him to reconcile all things to Himself, by Him, whether things on earth or things in heaven, having made peace through the blood of His cross.

And I believe that we, who once were alienated and enemies in our mind by wicked works, yet now He has reconciled in the body of His flesh through death, to present us holy, and blameless, and above reproach in His sight—if indeed we continue in the faith, grounded and steadfast, and are not moved away from the hope of the gospel which we have heard. Amen (Colossians 1:15–23).

Appendix C

Lesson Plans for "Ancient 'Secrets,' Alternative Christianities, and True Truth"

THE FOLLOWING pages show the lesson plans I used with my congregation as well as with the joint Vacation Bible School Adult Class in July 2006 with the two other congregations I surveyed. Readers have my permission to use these lessons in their congregations.

PART 1

While ironing a shirt one day, I reached for the can of starch but accidentally picked up a can of bug spray. It looked almost like the starch, but the end result was nearly disastrous. Christianity and Gnosticism have similar "look-alikeness," but the end results are totally different. (Read Hebrews 5:12–14 as an opener.)

Anticosmic Dualism

There are common themes that define ancient and modern Gnosticism. One of the major themes is what Hans Jonas designated as a "dualistic-anticosmic spirit."[1] For the gnostic, the original fall is not after the arrival of a good creation, but *before* the creation; thus this created order is a consequence of the fall.[2]

Therefore, God, good and pure, is not the cause of this creation. Philip Lee, in his book *Against the Protestant Gnostics*, notes: "The solution of the gnostic type—ancient, medieval and modern—is to remove from God (or from God beyond God) the stigma of creation."[3] So, to divorce God from creation, the gnostics held that through a series of devolving emanations came a divine being, far distant from God, who created the cosmos in rebellion.

Creation was marred from the beginning, and it has imperfection programmed into its genetic fiber. As *The Gospel of Philip* puts it: "The world came into being through error. The agent who made it wanted it to be imperishable and immortal. He failed. He came up with less than his desire. The world was never incorruptible, nor was its maker."[4]

Escaping Responsibility

The result of the gnostics' creating a vast distance between the God beyond God and this erroneous creation is that they are then allowed "to escape the world with impunity, for neither gnostics nor their God have any stake in it."[5]

1. Jonas, *Gnostic Religion*, 33.
2. Ibid., 63.
3. Lee, *Protestant Gnostics*, 9.
4. Barnstone and Meyer, *Gnostic Bible*, 286.
5. Lee, *Protestant Gnostics*, 9.

Therefore the gnostic dualism is also clearly anticosmic. To cite Jonas again: "The gnostic God is not merely extra-mundane and supra-mundane, but in his ultimate meaning contra-mundane."[6]

Escaping Physicality

If the cosmos and the creation are evil, what does that mean about our physical side? Is my body an evil prison house with the Real Me captured inside? Is my deliverance only to come if I can escape this blighted bag of dust and wing my flight to worlds unknown? In the recently published and hyped-up *Gospel of Judas*, Jesus is pictured as telling Judas that his mission is to deliver Jesus from his humanity: "But you will exceed all of them. For you will sacrifice the man that clothes me."[7] Then the footnote makes this statement, "The death of Jesus, with the assistance of Judas, is taken to be the liberation of the spiritual person within."[8] That means that Jesus himself needs saving. Therefore Jesus doesn't save anyone else but himself, and he then is a pattern of our self-salvation. Bart Erhman, in his attendant article to the *Gospel of Judas*, makes this clear when he writes, "Salvation comes only to those who learn how to escape this world and its material trappings."[9] And a little later he writes, "Salvation does not come by worshiping the God of this world or ac-

6. Jonas, *Gnostic Religion*, 251.
7. *Gospel of Judas*, 43.
8. Ibid., footnote 137.
9. Ehrman, "Christianity Turned," 85.

cepting his creation. It comes by denying this world and rejecting the body that binds us to it."[10]

But this anticosmic dualism can show up in unique ways. For example, in *The Da Vinci Code*, Dan Brown shows little regard for history. Even though he mentions one or two historical figures and an occasional historical item, his overarching stream is nonhistorical, or better yet, antihistorical. Let me give you one example (read *The Da Vinci Code*, 233).

What's important, in Dan Brown's *Da Vinci Code* world of fiction, is not the historical, but the antihistorical. But this is a regular aspect of Gnosticism. For example, what we read in the Gospel of Judas above.

The Biblical Answer

1. Remember the Bible's story, from Genesis to Revelation (from *protology* to *eschatology*).

2. Genesis 1–3 and Romans 8:18–25.

3. Remember your Christology ("Westminster Shorter Catechism" 21).

4. Remember your sacramental theology.

10. Ibid., 101.

PART 2

Alternative Textual Authorities

Another striking identifying item of the gnostic badge is the proliferation of alternative textual authorities. As Elaine Pagels boasts in her book, *The Gnostic Gospels*, the gnostic texts provide "a powerful alternative" to orthodox Christianity.[11]

The reason for an auxiliary source of textual authority in gnostic circles revolves around retelling the Jewish-Christian story in anticosmic dualistic ways. Lee points out: "What is not always recognized is that before there can be a deliberate escape from the real world into an alternately designed world, there first must be a deliberate escape from the real God to an alternately designed God. This, in fact, is the gnostic trick."[12]

To retell the story from Jewish-Christian procosmic monotheism, it becomes essential for gnostic Christianity to have alternative textual authorities. That source may be supplemental gospels like *The Gospel of Truth* or *The Gospel of Judas*.

Alternative Hermeneutics

But then another way gnostics reshape the story is by using a template of unique interpretations of the Christian Scriptures, as is brought out in two of Pagels's books: *The*

---

11. Pagels, *Gnostic Gospels*, 151.
12. Lee, *Protestant Gnostics*, 9.

Johannine Gospel in Gnostic Exegesis and *The Gnostic Paul: Gnostic Exegesis of the Pauline Letters.* In both instances Pagels clearly shows how Valentinian gnostics read the Christian Scriptures. In fact, Pagels shows how *gnosis* was the crucial interpretive lens for how they read all canonical Scripture: "Heracleon shares this understanding of 'context.' For him, as for Ptolemy, '*gnosis*,' and not the textual wording, furnishes the exegetical context."[13]

For Gnosticism both of these are critical, because of their essential desire to disconnect their alternate version of Christianity from any historical and creational moorings.

Spreading Suspicion

On the flip side of this equation of textual authority, Gnosticism also desires to shake up confidence in the authenticity of the Christian Scriptures themselves. Questioning the historical validity of the canonical Gospels is indispensable in this kind of enterprise. This agenda is clearly being promoted, for example, in *The Da Vinci Code*: "Constantine commissioned and financed a new Bible, which omitted those gospels that spoke of Christ's human traits and embellished those gospels that made him godlike. The earlier gospels were outlawed, gathered up, and burned."[14] And then on the next page, "'What I mean,' Teabing countered, 'is that almost everything our fathers taught us about Christ is false.'"[15] Again, just a few pages later, "'These are photocopies of the Nag Hammadi and Dead

13. Pagels, *Johannine Gospel*, 43.

14. Brown, *Da Vinci Code*, 234.

15. Ibid., 235.

Sea Scrolls, which I mentioned earlier,' Teabing said. 'The earliest Christian records. Troublingly, they do not match up with the gospels in the Bible.'"[16] Here, and elsewhere, Brown, through his characters, asserts that the gnostic Nag Hammadi library, discovered in the 1940s, is an earlier and better source of telling us who Jesus was and the story of the divine. And even though Brown doesn't make a scholarly case for it, he repeatedly has his characters deny the value, historical reliability, and authentic nature of the canonical Gospels. In the words of one of his characters, "the greatest story ever told is, in fact, the greatest story ever sold."[17]

Now, to summarize up to this point: It is important, if one is going to retell the Hebrew-Christian story in a gnostic fashion, to tear down the historical validity and accuracy of the canonical Scriptures, take liberties to reinterpret them in gnostic fashion, and to posit an opposing set of textual authorities.

The Pneumatic Authority

Having alternative written and didactic authorities is not enough, though. Underneath there lies another more subtle and dangerous aspect. This aspect is easily missed, but must be more emphatically answered. The gnostics' real primary authority is the divine *pneuma* within themselves. "But the *pneumaticos*, 'spiritual' man, who does not belong to any objective scheme, is above the law, beyond good and evil, and a law unto himself in the power of his 'knowledge.'"[18]

16. Ibid., 245–6.
17. Ibid., 267.
18. Jonas, *Gnostic Religion*, 334.

Pagels stresses this as well when she points out, "The disciple who comes to know himself can discover, then, what
even Jesus cannot teach," and so he becomes a follower of
his own mind. "He learns what he needs to know by himself
in meditative silence. Consequently, he considers himself
equal to everyone, maintaining his own independence of
everyone else's authority."[19] That means that whoever comes
to "see the Lord" by way of an inner vision "can claim that
his or her own authority equals, or surpasses, that of the
Twelve—and of their successors."[20] Therefore, what matters
to the gnostic is not the historicity of Jesus nor the historical authenticity of the canonical Gospels, nor any objective
authority, but "spiritual vision."[21] To put this another way,
the gnostic becomes her own authoritative text.

Does this kind of thing happen in Christian circles?
What are some ways it comes out on the left and on the
right?

How to Answer

First, "We don't know how exactly how many gospels were
written about Jesus in the first two hundred years or so of
Christianity. *The four in the New Testament are the oldest
ones to survive*."[22] Therefore, the canonical Gospels were
written within living memory,[23] whereas most, if not all,

19. Pagels, *Gnostic Gospels*, 131–32.

20. Ibid., 13–14.

21. Ibid., 11.

22. Ehrman, "Christianity Turned," 81. Emphasis mine.

23. Recently there was the last surviving soldier of a surprising
incident that happened in 1914: the Christmas Celebration. These

of the gnostic writings were written late second century to somewhere in the fourth century. They are unabashed fabrications, "what if" stories, simple dialogues, etc.

Second, Bart Ehrman has let the little kitten out of the bag: "The problem was that you couldn't reason with a gnostic to show him the error of his ways: He had secret knowledge that you didn't!"[24] Philip Jenkins puts his finger on the bias that makes this a difficult issue: "If the rediscovered gospel in question appeals to the tastes and interests of the modern readers, then that is all the authority the text requires. In a universe of extreme subjectivity, the whole question of 'but is it true?' is not only irrelevant, it is almost offensively naïve."[25]

The point is that the interpretive bifocal a person wears either opens her understanding or skews it. So how do you answer this? Tell the old, old story of Jesus and his love! Rehearse the creation account. Rehearse the fall and the curse that now rests on all creation. This was one of the main things folks like St. Irenaeus did as they confronted Gnosticism. They rehearsed the good creation from the good God—then fall—then curse—then redemption/resurrection/recreation story, and then they compared it to the gnostic cosmology.

Yet, as you tell the old, old story, remember the prejudice, the bias that underlies all of this. To quote Jenkins

---

incidents happened over ninety years ago, as we know from history and recorded testimonies. And at any moment this man could have challenged those recordings, and his having been there would have the been heavy weight on his side!

24. Ehrman, "Christianity Turned," 88.

25. Jenkins, *Hidden Gospels*, 89.

again: "The vastly exaggerated claims made on behalf of these gospels are more revealing about what contemporary scholars and writers would like to find about the first Christian ages, and how these ideas are communicated, accurately or otherwise, to a mass public. The alternative gospels are thus very important sources, . . . for what they tell us about the interest groups who seek to use them today."[26]

This would mean that you will have to attempt to draw their bias out into the full light. The goal of doing this is to expose and challenge their prejudices *qua* prejudices.

Questions to Work Through

1. Why is it important to challenge these prejudices and biases?

2. Why is it essential that the gnostic types have their suspiciousness thrown back into their own faces?

3. Why do we push the canonical Gospels as historically, authentically, and authoritatively genuine?

4. In what way(s) is this of utmost importance—not only as you answer gnostics, but in our Christian faith?

5. What resources might be helpful as you pursue establishing the historical and authoritative genuineness of the New Testament Gospels?

26. Ibid., 5.

PART 3

God

Along with establishing alternative sources of authority is the gnostic understanding of God. This is what Lee called the gnostic trick—the escaping from the real God by manufacturing an alternative God.[27] In removing the "Father of truth" far from creation, the gnostics placed another god in between the perfect god and the devil. The in-between god is described by Ptolemy, a second-century A.D. gnostic, in his Letter to Flora, as "neither good nor evil and unjust" but an arbitrator of a justice that depends on him.[28] Between the good god and the creator god, there is also a whole gaggle of aeons and divine entities emanating from the good god and working fairly independently of the good god and one another.

Surprisingly, in the midst of all the divine entities is the divine Man. For example, Pagels draws a picture for her readers of the god, who is the primal *Anthropos.*[29] And this primal *Anthropos* is really humanity, which is god-over-all.[30] Hans Jonas refers to this as well when he writes, "To the Gnostics the existence of a pre-cosmic god 'Man' expressed one of the major secrets of their Knowledge, and some sects even went so far as to call the highest godhead

27. Lee, *Protestant Gnostics*, 9.
28. Barnstone and Meyer, *Gnostic Bible*, 305.
29. Pagels, *Gnostic Gospels*, 122–23.
30. Ibid., 144.

himself 'Man.'"[31] This means, then, that there is a very real identification between the divine and humankind. In Pagels's words:

> What differentiated them (Orthodox and gnostics) was the level of their understanding. Uninitiated Christians mistakenly worshiped the creator, as if he were God; they believed in Christ as the one who would save them from sin, and who they believed had risen bodily from the dead: they accepted him by faith, but without understanding the mystery of his nature—or their own. But those who had gone on to receive gnosis had come to recognize Christ as the one sent from the Father of truth, whose coming revealed to them that their own nature was identical with his—and with God's.[32]

The Gnostic Jesus

Christ is no more divine than we are in essence. Our natures are identical, so that when we achieve gnosis we find that we are really Christ's twin: "But those who had gone on to receive gnosis had come to recognize Christ as the one sent from the Father of Truth, whose coming revealed to them that their own nature was identical with his—and with God's."[33] This brings her to point out that once we achieve gnosis, we no longer see ourselves as Christian, but

31. Ibid., 217.
32. Ibid., 116.
33. Ibid.

as Christ.[34] By pursuing this gnostic version of the divine, Pagels has thrown out the otherness of God, the *I–Thou* distinctive, so that the gnostic can now say, *I am Thou.* This strips Christ of having been and continuing to be "God and man, in two distinct natures, and one person forever."[35]

Jesus is more of an educator than a savior. In *The Gospel of Judas*, Jesus is pictured as telling Judas that his mission is to deliver Jesus from his humanity: "But you will exceed all of them. For you will sacrifice the man that clothes me."[36] Then the footnote makes this statement, "The death of Jesus, with the assistance of Judas, is taken to be the liberation of the spiritual person within."[37]

Only part of Jesus escapes (a very key word!) this cosmic trash-heap. The gnostic writing called *The Book of Baruch* declares, "Jesus left his body to Edem[38] by the tree and ascended to the Good. He said to her, 'Woman, here is your son.' He left his soul and earthly body, but his spirit he placed in the hands of the father[39] and then ascended to the Good."[40]

Therefore, Jesus' death is actually his liberation from this cosmic trash-heap. That being the case, Jesus doesn't need to be physically raised from the dead, because that

34. Ibid., 134.
35. *Westminster Shorter Catechism*, 21.
36. *Gospel of Judas*, 43.
37. Ibid., footnote 137.
38. Edem is mother, soul, and breath, who breathes soul into Adam.
39. Father is *Elohim*, who breathes spirit into the firstborn Adam.
40. Barnstone and Meyer, *Gnostic Bible*, 132.

would be a re-enslavement of the divine being. Erhman makes this very clear:

> The need is to escape this world and its creator. That happens once one relinquishes the body that belongs to the creator. Jesus' death is his own escape. And when we die, we too can escape. . . . There will be no resurrection. This is perhaps the key point of all. Jesus will not be raised from the dead in this book.[41] Why would he be? The entire point of salvation is to *escape* this material world. A resurrection of the dead corpse brings the person back *into* the world of the creator. Since the point is to allow the soul to leave this world behind and to enter into 'that great and holy generation'—that is, the divine realm that transcends this world—a resurrection of the body is the very last thing that Jesus, or any of his true followers, would want.[42]

Summary of This Section

What does all this mean? As we have already noted, in the gnostic framework, creation and our physicality are a result of the fall and thus intrinsically rotten. The god of the Old Testament is a mean *hombre*, and we need to get around him, one way or the other, so that our spirits can reach the *pleroma*, or place of the good God's fullness. All of these things we have already discussed.

41. *Gospel of Judas.*
42. Ehrman, "Christianity Turned," 110.

So what else does the gnostic notion of God mean? As someone insightfully said to me once, "If all of us are special, then none of us are special." If we are really on par with Jesus, then we are either as divine as he, or he is in need of as much salvation as we! That is why Bart Ehrman writes, "But some of us are trapped divinities. And we need to learn how to return to our heavenly home."[43]

How to Answer

1. We must see that biblically, the place of Jesus is similar but distinctly different from us. Follow Colossians 1:15–23, which Paul rehearses in the face of an embryonic form of gnosticism.

2. Rehearse the gospel, especially the importance laid on the physical, historical death, burial, and resurrection of Christ.

3. Reclaim the pattern of St. Irenaeus's arguments in his five-volume work *Against Heresies.*

43. Ibid., 87.

PART 4

*"Unable to preach Christ and him crucified,
we preach humanity and it improved."*[44]

Gnostic Salvation

The idea of salvation assumes that there is something to be rescued from and something to be delivered to. To understand gnostic salvation, it might be helpful to ask the four worldview questions described by J. Richard Middleton and Brian Walsh in their book, *Truth is Stranger Than It Used to Be: Biblical Faith in a Postmodern Age.*

Who are we? Because the created order is the work of a lesser divine being, and the creation of our human physicality the work of the Archons (the powers that rule over the world under the demiurge or creator God), and because creation is a result of a precosmic fall, we are imprisoned creatures. The Archons created our humanity in order to keep the divine substance of the *pneuma* captive.[45] Or even more clearly, Bart Erhman writes, "But some of us are trapped divinities. And we need to learn how to return to our heavenly home."[46]

Where are we? Our existence is hedged in by a marred creation, a creation that is part of the alienation between "the Father of truth" and humankind. "The universe, the domain of the Archons, is like a vast prison whose inner-

---

44. Willimon, *Peculiar Speech*, 9.
45. Jonas, *Gnostic Religion*, 44.
46. Ehrman, "Christianity Turned," 87.

most dungeon is the earth, the scene of man's life."[47] The cosmos in which we live was created by the *demiurge* rather than the God over all. This demiurge is often equated with the Old Testament God.

What is wrong? Estrangement is the key to the gnostic understanding of what is wrong. Humankind is simultaneously with God and alienated from the world, and yet because of the world, humankind and God are separated from one another.[48] As noted above, the Archons have encased the *pneuma* in the human body and drugged this divine *pneuma* so that it sleeps, or stays permanently in ignorance of what it is and where it belongs. The Archons are also barring the way so that souls that seek to climb up to God are kept from escaping the world and returning to God.[49] This is bad news for the cosmos, because the cosmos is the main part of the problem. Therefore God's reaction to the cosmos is not going to be pretty; "The gnostic God is not merely extra-mundane and supra-mundane, but in his ultimate meaning contra-mundane."[50]

What is the solution? The gnostic answer is multilayered. In one way, the real goal or focus of salvation is the divine: "And the real object of salvation is the godhead itself, its theme the divine integrity."[51] The idea is the "ultimate salvation of what is divine in the world and humanity."[52] Salvation time will be when "all the pneumatic elements in

---

47. Jonas, *Gnostic Religion*, 43.

48. Ibid., 326.

49. Ibid., 43.

50. Ibid., 251.

51. Ibid., 196.

52. Barnstone and Meyer, *Gnostic Bible*, 16.

the world have been 'formed' by knowledge and perfected."[53] The dualistic present will then collapse into a monad of divine existence.

At another level, salvation is the awakening of the divine spark within, attaining the enlightenment. As Marvin Meyer writes in his introduction to *The Gospel of Judas*, "For gnostics, the fundamental problem in human life is not sin but ignorance, and the best way to address this problem is not through faith but through knowledge."[54]

Therefore, the emphasis on gnosis, or "knowledge," is the essence of gnostic salvation: the "knowledge of God and the essential oneness of the self with God."[55] A glimpse of this gnostic salvation is caught in *The Da Vinci Code* when Langdon is reminiscing about one of his university classes he taught at Harvard. He is explaining the divine union in sex: "The next time you find yourself with a woman, look in your heart and see if you cannot approach sex as a mystical, spiritual act. Challenge yourself to find that spark of divinity that man can only achieve through union with the sacred feminine."[56] But this saving knowledge is a direct, "unmediated mystical knowledge."[57]

Finally, if God is contra-mundane, if the cosmos and the created are a main part of the problem, then they must be escaped altogether. Therefore, it is no surprise that the Jesus of *The Gospel of Judas* needs to be saved from his humanity. Jesus reportedly gives permission for Judas to

53. Jonas, *Gnostic Religion*, 196.

54. 7.

55. Ibid., 5.

56. Brown, *Da Vinci Code*, 310.

57. Barnstone and Meyer, *Gnostic Bible*, 16.

betray him so as to free him; "But you will exceed all of them. For you will sacrifice the man that clothes me."[58] This is born out in the footnote that accompanies this text; "The death of Jesus, with the assistance of Judas, is taken to be the liberation of the spiritual person within."[59] If this is the case with Jesus, it is just as necessary for his followers. As Bart Ehrman notes in his article that accompanies *The Gospel of Judas*, "We are trapped here, in these bodies of flesh, and we need to learn how to escape."[60] And a little later on, Ehrman declares unashamedly, "Salvation does not come by worshiping the God of this world or accepting his creation. It comes by denying this world and rejecting the body that binds us to it."[61] This is why there will be no resurrection, why Jesus would not want to be raised from the dead, and neither should we.[62]

To bring this to a conclusion, here is a telling observation from David Mills of *Touchstone Magazine*: "That a system such as Gnosticism explains so much is a good part of its appeal. It claims to replace faith—and a delusionary faith at that—with knowledge."[63]

How to Answer

When J. Gresham Machen, the Professor of New Testament at Princeton Seminary, was fighting for the life of the

58. *Gospel of Judas*, 43.
59. Ibid., footnote 137.
60. Ehrman, "Christianity Turned," 84.
61. Ibid., 101.
62. Ibid., 110.
63. Mills, "Getting Jesus Right," no pages.

Presbyterian Church (USA) in the 1920s, he wrote a book in which he contrasted two religions. Both religions claimed to be Christian. On the one hand, there was orthodox Christianity, which was based on the Scriptures of the Old and New Testaments, the historical Jesus who was what the Nicene Creed said he was, and his message as recorded in the New Testament. On the other hand, Machen perceived that there was another religion in the Christian church that was strangling orthodox Christianity. This religion was covering itself with the Christian language and using Christian words and symbols. However, it was denying the recognized and historical meanings of those words and symbols and reinvesting them with utterly different meanings. This other religion sought to defang the Christian faith by denying the historical and authentic authority of the canonical gospels, as well as to turn Christianity into a religion of ethics. But the ethical norms were to be broad and concessive to the modern moment. The book he wrote laying all of this out was *Christianity and Liberalism*, which was published in 1923.

Machen pointed to many aspects of this conflict between the two religions of orthodox Christianity and liberalism, most of which are relevant for the present ecclesiastical scene. In the second chapter of the book, he writes about doctrine. In this chapter he elucidates an underlying principle that echoes throughout his book, is an undercurrent in this work, and is pronouncedly present in the survey questions. The underlying assumption is that the Christian faith is a historical faith. If it could be proved that there never was the Jesus of the canonical gospels, then there would be no Christian faith. Whatever came out of that discovery would be some other religion.

In clear and uncompromising words, Machen wrote, "The Christian movement at its inception was not a way of life in the modern sense, but a way of life founded upon a message. It was based, not upon mere feeling, not upon a mere program of work, but upon an account of facts. In other words it was based upon doctrine."[64]

Any form of Christianity that has placed its emphasis on ethics ("orthopraxy") without the foundation of the real, historical, doctrinal truth of orthodoxy has fallen off into the world of another religion:

> The liberal preacher is really rejecting the whole basis of Christianity, which is religion founded not on aspirations, but on facts. Here is found the most fundamental difference between liberalism and Christianity—liberalism is altogether in the imperative mood, while Christianity begins with a triumphant indicative; liberalism appeals to man's will, while Christianity announces, first, a gracious act of God.[65]

What Machen is pointing to is seen by Pope Benedict XVI in our pluralistic world, where "Ethos without logos cannot endure."[66] The truth is that creed and deed are not opposites, as some in the modern Evangelical church are purporting as they tout their second Reformation of *Deeds not Creeds*. Instead, the very source of our deeds are the true truths we believe. Again, as Pope Benedict XVI wrote:

64. Machen, *Christianity and Liberalism*, 21.

65. Ibid., 27.

66. Benedict, *Pilgrim Fellowship*, 262.

"Belief and sacrament remain constitutive for the Church. Otherwise she just gets lost. And then she no longer has anything to offer mankind. She draws her life from the Logos having become flesh, from the truth having become the way."[67]

Therefore, Machen's point is that to make aspirations or feelings the ground of our faith is to strip it of teeth and life. Machen was not denying the place of experience or ethics, but as he clearly drives the point home repeatedly, they must be founded on historical fact and doctrine: "According to the Christian conception, a creed is not a mere expression of the Christian experience, but on the contrary it is a setting forth of those facts upon which experience is based."[68]

As I stated earlier, Machen's point is one of the main undercurrents of this work and the survey questions. If Gnosticism is grounded on anticosmic dualism, history means little to nothing. All that matters is my personal experience of having the inner vision of "the living Christ." Christianity's remedy to this challenge is to rehearse the truth of history and doctrine. Machen puts it succinctly, "'Christ died'—that is history; 'Christ died for our sins'— that is doctrine. Without these two elements, joined in an absolutely indissoluble union, there is no Christianity."[69]

67. Ibid., 264.

68. Machen, *Christianity and Liberalism*, 19.

69. Ibid., 27.

PART 5

What has been the goal of this series of studies? In the words of Hebrews, "For though by this time you ought to be teachers, you need someone to teach you again the basic principles of the oracles of God. You need milk, not solid food, for everyone who lives on milk is unskilled in the word of righteousness, since he is a child. But solid food is for the mature, for those who have their powers of discernment trained by constant practice to distinguish good from evil" (Hebrews 5:12–14 ESV).

The key is discernment: learning to discern, recognize, detect, and spot the spirits who are trying to commandeer your allegiance.

Coupled with the goal of discernment must be love—a love that builds up fellow believers and a love for God, both of which flow out of our being known by God. As the Apostle Paul wrote, "Knowledge (gnosis) puffs up, but love edifies. And if anyone thinks that he knows anything, he knows nothing yet as he ought to know. But if anyone loves God, this one is known by Him" (1 Corinthians 8:1b–3).

All doctrine and biblical education must be to enrich our knowledge, but it must always be for the purpose of leading us to a richer, fuller love for God in Jesus Christ. As Paul points out in other places, love for God in Jesus Christ is fleshed out in our love for one another. If our so-called knowledge leads us to exalt our ego or our importance at the expense of Christ and Christ's church, then we have begun falling down the gnostic staircase into the dark dungeon of self-destruction at the bottom—and we may be liable for dragging others with us. Take notice of the elitists on the left ("We're the new wave of Christians, we're the more enlightened"), on the right ("We have the dogma down pat and don't need anyone to teach us"), and in the middle ("We're the superior middle-of-the-road, we know better than to be fundamentalists or flaming liberals! We're better than them both").

Role-Play Exercise

Instructions: This section is a crucial conclusion to the lessons. The teacher should play the "gnostic" role and call on someone in the audience to sit next to them and be the "friend." The gnostic then makes the statement and the friend should respond, catching the gnostic trend and steering the gnostic toward the remedy learned in these lessons. Once the scene is over, allow for a short, open discussion permitting the audience to chime in with perceptions and other possible answers. Then move on to the next scene until finished. Every time I have done this class, this role-play section is when my audience has gotten it and enthusiastically acknowledged that they have finally understood the importance of the class.

1st scene: Gnostic—"All of the historical gospel stuff is fine, but I really like *The Gospel of Thomas*. In fact, we had a doctor teach that writing—*The Gospel of Thomas*—for two years at our church. It's really comforting to know that I already have everything in me I need to get back to god. In fact, I really feel so much better knowing that Christ and I are like, well, like twins. I'm as divine as Christ, and that book helped me to recover my feeling of union with god."

2nd scene: Gnostic—"You know, that god in the Old Testament seems pretty mean. Like when he tells Israel to stone to death people who disagree with him. I'm really glad that Jesus told us about the God of love. I can handle that Jesus love–stuff better!"

3rd scene: Gnostic—"I'm really not feeling too well. This cancer has really gotten hold of me, and is giving me all kinds of trouble. You know, I just want to die. I have thought about going to Oregon and getting one of those doctors to just let my spirit go. I'd be in a happier place. And who cares about this old body anyway? It's just so much dust and trash. I just want to be free and go be with God."

Bibliography

Adeyemo, Tokunboh. "Jude." In *Africa Bible Commentary*, edited by Tokunboh Adeyemo, 1565–68. Grand Rapids: Zondervan, 2006.

Barnstone, Willis, and Marvin W. Meyer, eds. *The Gnostic Bible*. 1st ed. Boston: Shambhala, 2003.

Barton, Bruce B., et al. *1 & 2 Peter and Jude*. Life Application Bible Commentary Series. Wheaton, IL: Tyndale House, 1995.

Behr, John. "The Demonstration of the Apostolic Preaching." In *St. Irenaeus of Lyons: On the Apostolic Preaching*, 7–26. Crestwood, NY: St. Vladimir's Seminary Press, 1997.

———. *The Mystery of Christ: Life in Death*. Crestwood, NY: St. Vladimir's Seminary Press, 2006.

Benedict, Pope XIV, et al. *Pilgrim Fellowship of Faith: The Church as Communion*. San Francisco: Ignatius, 2005.

Benedict, Pope XVI. *Jesus of Nazareth*. 7th ed. New York: Doubleday, 2007.

———. Truth and Tolerance: *Christian Belief and World Religions*. San Francisco: Ignatius, 2004.

Billings, J. Todd. *Calvin, Participation, and the Gift: The Activity of Believers in Union with Christ*. Changing Paradigms in Historical and Systematic Theology. Oxford: Oxford University Press, 2007.

———. "John Calvin: United to God through Christ." In *Partakers of the Divine Nature: The History and Development of Deification in the Christian Traditions*, edited by Michael J. Christensen and Jeffery A. Wittung, 200–218. Grand Rapids: Baker Academic, 2007.

———. *The Word of God for the People of God: An Entryway to the Theological Interpretation of Scripture*. Grand Rapids: Eerdmans, 2010.

Bloom, Harold. *The American Religion: The Emergence of the Post-Christian Nation*. New York: Simon & Schuster, 1992.

Blum, Edwin A. "Jude." In *The Expositor's Bible Commentary: With the New International Version of the Holy Bible*, edited by Frank Ely Gaebelein and J. D. Douglas, 381–96. Vol. 12. Grand Rapids: Zondervan, 1981.

Bobrinskoy, Boris. *The Mystery of the Trinity: Trinitarian Experience and Vision in the Biblical and Patristic Tradition*. Crestwood, NY: St. Vladimir's Seminary Press, 1999.

Boersma, Hans. *Violence, Hospitality, and the Cross: Reappropriating the Atonement Tradition*. Grand Rapids: Baker Academic, 2004.

The Book of Church Order of the Presbyterian Church in America. 6th ed. June 2003. The Office of the Stated Clerk of the General Assembly of the Presbyterian Church in America, 8 January 2005.

The Book of Common Prayer and Administration of the Sacraments and Other Rites and Ceremonies of the Church. Episcopal Church. New York: Church Hymnal Corp., 1979.

Bromiley, Geoffrey William. *Children of Promise: The Case for Baptizing Infants*. Grand Rapids: Eerdmans, 1996.

———. *Sacramental Teaching and Practice in the Reformation Churches*. Grand Rapids: Eerdmans, 1957.

Brown, Dan. *The Da Vinci Code: A Novel*. 1st ed. New York: Doubleday, 2003.

Calvin, Jean, et al. *Institutes of the Christian Religion*. 7th ed. Philadelphia: Presbyterian Board of Christian Education, 1936.

Calvin, John. *Institutes of the Christian Religion*. (1559) 1845. http://www.reformed.org/books/institutes/index.html.

Chan, Simon. *Spiritual Theology: A Systematic Study of the Christian Life*. Downers Grove, IL: InterVarsity, 1998.

Chapell, Bryan. *Christ-Centered Preaching: Redeeming the Expository Sermon*. Grand Rapids: Baker Books, 1994.

Clowney, Edmund P. *The Church*. Contours of Christian Theology. Downers Grove, IL: InterVarsity, 1995.

Dabney, Robert Lewis. *Evangelical Eloquence: A Course of Lectures on Preaching*. Carlisle, PA: Banner of Truth Trust, 1999.

Dawn, Marva J. *A Royal Waste of Time: The Splendor of Worshiping God and Being Church for the World*. Grand Rapids: Eerdmans, 1999.

Ehrman, Bart D. "Christianity Turned on Its Head: The Alternative Vision of the Gospel of Judas." In *The Gospel of Judas*, edited by Rodolphe Kasser et al., 77–120. Washington DC: National Geographic Society, 2006.

"Epistle to Diognetus." In *The Apostolic Fathers*, edited by Bart D. Ehrman. Vol. 2. Loeb Classical Library 25. Cambridge, MA: Harvard University Press, 2003.

Erickson, Millard J. *Christian Theology*. Grand Rapids: Baker, 1985.

Ferguson, Sinclair B. *The Holy Spirit: Contours of Christian Theology*. Downers Grove, IL: InterVarsity, 1996.

Frame, John M. *Apologetics to the Glory of God: An Introduction*. Phillipsburg, NJ: P&R, 1994.

Frend, W. H. C. *The Rise of Christianity*. Philadelphia: Fortress, 1984.

The Gospel of Judas. Ed. Rodolphe Kasser et al. Washington DC: National Geographic Society, 2006.

"The Gospel of Philip." In *The Gnostic Bible*, edited by Willis Barnstone and Marvin Meyer, 257–98. Boston: Shambala, 2003.

"The Gospel of Truth." In *The Gnostic Bible*, edited by Willis Barnstone and Marvin Meyer, 239–56. Boston: Shambala, 2003.

Grant, Robert McQueen. *Irenaeus of Lyons*. The Early Church Fathers. New York: Routledge, 1997.

Guthrie, Donald. *New Testament Theology*. Downers Grove, IL: InterVarsity, 1981.

Hart, D. G. *Deconstructing Evangelicalism: Conservative Protestantism in the Age of Billy Graham*. Grand Rapids: Baker Academic, 2004.

———. *Recovering Mother Kirk: The Case for Liturgy in the Reformed Tradition*. Grand Rapids: Baker Academic, 2003.

The Heidelberg Catechism. Sioux Falls, SD: Pine Hill, 1992.

Hoekema, Anthony. "Heaven: Not Just an Eternal Day Off." *Christianity Today*, 2003. http://www.ctlibrary.com/ct/2003/juneweb-only/6-2-54.0.html.

Irenaeus. "A Refutation and Subversion of Knowledge Falsely So Called." In *The Ante-Nicene Fathers: Translations of the Writings of the Fathers Down to A.D. 325*, edited by Alexander Roberts, James Donaldson, and A. Cleveland Coxe, 309–578. Vol. 1. Grand Rapids: Eerdmans, 1951.

Irenaeus, and Hans Urs von Balthasar, ed. *The Scandal of the Incarnation: Irenaeus against the Heresies*. San Francisco: Ignatius, 1990.

James, P. D. *Death in Holy Orders*. New York: Ballantine, 2007.

Jenkins, Philip. *Hidden Gospels: How the Search for Jesus Lost Its Way*. Oxford: Oxford University Press, 2001.

Jensen, Peter. *The Revelation of God*. Contours of Christian Theology. Downers Grove, IL: InterVarsity, 2002.

Jensen, Phillip D., and Tony Payne. *Two Ways to Live: Know and Share the Gospel*. Participant's manual. Kingsford NSW, Australia: Matthias Media, 2003.

———. *Two Ways to Live: The Choice We All Face*. Pocket edition. Kingsford NSW, Australia: Matthias Media, 2003.

Jonas, Hans. *The Gnostic Religion: The Message of the Alien God and the Beginnings of Christianity*. 3rd ed. Boston: Beacon, 2001.

Kasser, Rodolphe, Marvin Meyer, and Gregor Wurst, eds. *The Gospel of Judas: From Codex Tchacos*. Washington DC: National Geographic, 2006.

Kelly, J. N. D. *A Commentary on the Epistles of Peter and of Jude*. Black's New Testament Commentaries. A & C Black, 1969.

King, Karen L. *What Is Gnosticism?* London: Belknap, 2003.

Ladd, George Eldon, and Donald Alfred Hagner. *A Theology of the New Testament*. Rev. ed. Grand Rapids: Eerdmans, 1993.

Lawson, Steven J. *Famine in the Land: A Passionate Call for Expository Preaching*. Chicago: Moody Press, 2003.

Lee, Philip J. *Against the Protestant Gnostics*. Oxford: Oxford University Press, 1993.

———. "Protestant Gnosticism Reconsidered." *Modern Reformation* 17 (2008) 37–40.

Lloyd-Jones, David Martyn. *Preaching and Preachers*. Grand Rapids: Zondervan, 1971.

———. *Spiritual Depression: Its Causes and Cure*. Grand Rapids: Eerdmans, 1965.

Machen, J. Gresham. *Christianity and Liberalism*. Grand Rapids: Eerdmans, 1923.

Macleod, Donald. *From Glory to Golgotha: Controversial Issues in the Life of Christ*. Fearn: Christian Focus, 2002.

McGrath, Alister E. *Christian Theology: An Introduction*. 3rd ed. Oxford: Blackwell, 2001.

Meyer, Marvin. "Introduction." In *The Gospel of Judas*, edited by Rodolphe Kasser et al., 1–16. Washington DC: National Geographic Society, 2006.

———. "Judas and the Gnostic Connection." In *The Gospel of Judas*, edited by Rodolphe Kasser et al., 137–70. Washington DC: National Geographic, 2006.

Mills, David. "Getting Jesus Right." *Touchstone Magazine: A Journal of Mere Christianity*. October 2001. http://www.touchstonemag.com/archives/article.php?id=14-08-022-f.

Morris, Leon. *Testaments of Love: A Study of Love in the Bible*. Grand Rapids: Eerdmans, 1981.

Nazianzus, Gregory. "To Cledonius against Appollinarius (Epistle 101)." In *Christology of the Later Fathers*, edited by Edward Rochie Hardy, 111–232. Philadelphia: Westminster John Knox, 1954.

Newbigin, Lesslie. *The Gospel in a Pluralist Society*. Grand Rapids: Eerdmans, 1989.

———. *Proper Confidence: Faith, Doubt, and Certainty in Christian Discipleship*. Grand Rapids: Eerdmans, 1995.

Osborn, Eric Francis. *Irenaeus of Lyons*. Cambridge: Cambridge University Press, 2001.

Pagels, Elaine H. *Beyond Belief: The Secret Gospel of Thomas*. 1st ed. New York: Vintage, 2004.

———. *The Gnostic Gospels*. 1st ed. New York: Vintage, 1989.

———. *The Gnostic Paul: Gnostic Exegesis of the Pauline Letters*. Harrisburg: Trinity, 1992.

———. *The Johannine Gospel in Gnostic Exegesis: Heracleon's Commentary on John*. Atlanta: Scholars, 1989.

———. *The Origin of Satan*. 1st ed. New York: Vintage, 1996.

Peterson, Eugene H. *Christ Plays in Ten Thousand Places: A Conversation in Spiritual Theology*. Grand Rapids: Eerdmans, 2005.

Plato, and C. C. W. Taylor. *Protagoras*. The World's Classics. New York: Oxford University Press, 1996.

Reno, R. R., *Genesis*. Brazos Theological Commentary of the Bible. Grand Rapids: Brazos, 2010.

Ridderbos, Herman N., and Richard B. Gaffin. *Redemptive History and the New Testament Scriptures*. Biblical & Theological Studies. 2nd rev. ed. Phillipsburg, NJ: Presbyterian and Reformed, 1988.

Smith, Christian, and Melinda Lundquist Denton. *Soul Searching: The Religious and Spiritual Lives of American Teenagers*. Oxford: Oxford University Press, 2005.

Stoker, Bram. *Dracula*. New York: Barnes & Noble Classics, 2003.

Strobel, Lee. *The Case for Christmas: A Journalist Investigates the Identity of the Child in the Manger*. Grand Rapids: Zondervan, 2005.

Tertullian. "The Prescriptions against the Heretics." In *Early Latin Theology; Selections from Tertullian, Cyprian, Ambrose, and Jerome*, edited by S. L. Greenslade, 31–64. Vol. 5. The Library of Christian Classics. Philadelphia: Westminster John Knox, 1956.

Thompson, Bard. *Liturgies of the Western Church*. Living Age Books. Cleveland: Meridian Books, 1961.

Torrance, Thomas Forsyth. *The Trinitarian Faith: The Evangelical Theology of the Ancient Catholic Church*. Edinburgh: T & T Clark, 1997.

Watson, Duane F. "The Letter of Jude: Introduction, Commentary, and Reflections." In *The New Interpreter's Bible: A Commentary in Twelve Volumes*, edited by Leander E. Keck, 473–99. Vol. 12. Nashville: Abingdon, 1998.

"Westminster Confession of Faith." *Westminster Confession of Faith, the Larger and Shorter Catechisms*. Glasgow: Free Presbyterian, 1995.

Wilken, Todd. "The Promise-Driven Church." *Modern Reformation* 14 (2005) 20–24.

Willimon, William H. *Peculiar Speech: Preaching to the Baptized*. Grand Rapids: Eerdmans, 1992.

Wright, N. T. *The Challenge of Jesus: Rediscovering Who Jesus Was and Is*. Downers Grove, IL: InterVarsity, 1999.

———. *Judas and the Gospel of Jesus: Have We Missed the Truth About Christianity?* Grand Rapids: Baker, 2006.

———. *The Last Word: Beyond the Bible Wars to a New Understanding of the Authority of Scripture*. 1st ed. San Francisco: HarperSanFrancisco, 2005.

———. *The New Testament and the People of God*. Christian Origins and the Question of God. Vol 1. Minneapolis: Fortress, 1992.

———. *Paul: In Fresh Perspective*. Minneapolis: Fortress, 2005.

———. *Who Was Jesus?* Grand Rapids: Eerdmans, 1993.

Zerwick, Max, and Mary Grosvenor. *A Grammatical Analysis of the Greek New Testament*. Unabridged, 5th rev. ed. Rome: Pontificio Istituto Biblico, 1996.

Subject/Name Index

Lightning Source UK Ltd.
Milton Keynes UK
UKOW06f0807060716

277735UK00001B/31/P

9 781610 974141